NEW MEXICO WILDLIFE VIEWING GUIDE

Jane S. MacCarter

FALCON™

Helena, Montana

Author and State Project Manager:
Jane S. MacCarter

New Mexico State Project Leader:
Don L. MacCarter

National Watchable Wildlife Program Manager:
Kate Davies, Defenders of Wildlife

Original Illustrations:
Jennifer Dewey

Front cover photo:
Immature bald eagle, Don L. MacCarter

Back cover photos:
Cimarron Canyon, Mark Nohl/New Mexico Dept. of Tourism
Bull elk, Don L. MacCarter

ACKNOWLEDGMENTS

Special thanks for the collective expertise, patience, and support of the following individuals and organizations on behalf of the New Mexico Watchable Wildlife Project. Heartfelt gratitude is also extended to the many site managers and other experts who helped provide information and copy review.

State Steering Committee

Kevin Bixby, New Mexico State Land Office; Scott Brown, New Mexico Dept. of Game & Fish; Frank Bryce, U. S. Fish & Wildlife Service; Bill Dixon, New Mexico Wildlife Foundation; Leon Fager, USDA Forest Service; David Henderson, Randall Davey Audubon Center; David Johnson, New Mexico Park & Recreation Division; Glen Kaye, National Park Service; Barbara Masinton, Bureau of Land Management; John Nitzel, New Mexico Dept. of Highways and Transportation; Terry Sullivan, The Nature Conservancy; Bruce Thompson, New Mexico State University; Gail Tunberg, USDA Forest Service; Claire Tyrpak, Share With Wildlife (NMDGF)

Special Thanks to the following individuals for their invaluable assistance: Bob Bavin, John Hubbard, Dan Beck, Kathy McKim, Nancy Bennett, Greg Medina, Mark Birkhauser, Leslie Milton, Kendall Clark , Charlie Painter, Ralph J. Fisher, Catherine Sandell, Bill Hays, Greg Schmidt

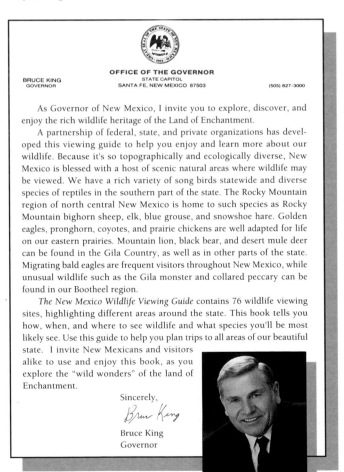

OFFICE OF THE GOVERNOR
STATE CAPITOL
SANTA FE, NEW MEXICO 87503

BRUCE KING
GOVERNOR

(505) 827-3000

As Governor of New Mexico, I invite you to explore, discover, and enjoy the rich wildlife heritage of the Land of Enchantment.

A partnership of federal, state, and private organizations has developed this viewing guide to help you enjoy and learn more about our wildlife. Because it's so topographically and ecologically diverse, New Mexico is blessed with a host of scenic natural areas where wildlife may be viewed. We have a rich variety of song birds statewide and diverse species of reptiles in the southern part of the state. The Rocky Mountain region of north central New Mexico is home to such species as Rocky Mountain bighorn sheep, elk, blue grouse, and snowshoe hare. Golden eagles, pronghorn, coyotes, and prairie chickens are well adapted for life on our eastern prairies. Mountain lion, black bear, and desert mule deer can be found in the Gila Country, as well as in other parts of the state. Migrating bald eagles are frequent visitors throughout New Mexico, while unusual wildlife such as the Gila monster and collared peccary can be found in our Bootheel region.

The New Mexico Wildlife Viewing Guide contains 76 wildlife viewing sites, highlighting different areas around the state. This book tells you how, when, and where to see wildlife and what species you'll be most likely see. Use this guide to help you plan trips to all areas of our beautiful state. I invite New Mexicans and visitors alike to use and enjoy this book, as you explore the "wild wonders" of the land of Enchantment.

Sincerely,

Bruce King
Governor

CONTENTS

Copyright © 1994 by Falcon Press Publishing Co., Inc.,
Helena and Billings, MT.
Illustrations copyright © 1994 by Defenders of Wildlife.
Published in cooperation with Defenders of Wildlife.

Defenders of Wildlife and its design are registered
marks of Defenders of Wildlife, Washington, D.C.

All rights reserved, including the right to reproduce this
book or any part thereof in any form, except brief quotations
for reviews, without the written permission of the publisher.

Design, typesetting, and other prepress work by Falcon Press Helena, Montana.

Printed in the United States of America.

Cataloging-in Publication Data
MacCarter, Jane S.
      New Mexico wildlife viewing guide / Jane S. MacCarter.
            p. cm.
      Includes index.
      ISBN 1-56044-213-1
      1. Wildlife viewing sites — New Mexico -- Guidebooks. 2. Wildlife
watching -- New Mexico -- Guidebooks. I. Title.
QL 194.M33   1993
591.9789—dc20
                                                    93-42965
                                                    CIP

PROJECT SPONSORS

NEW MEXICO DEPARTMENT OF GAME AND FISH works on behalf of the viability of all wildlife species, living in a free-ranging and self-supporting state within their habitats in New Mexico. The Department encourages, manages for and supports the enjoyment, appreciation, and economic, scientific, and recreational use of our wildlife and their habitats. Support the Department's wildlife conservation efforts by means of the Share With Wildlife tax check-off program, the Project WILD education program, or by purchasing the Wildlife Conservation Stamp. For more information, contact New Mexico Department of Game and Fish, Villagra Building, Santa Fe, NM 87503 (505) 827-7911.

The USDA FOREST SERVICE has a mandate to protect, improve, and wisely use the nation's forest and range resources for multiple purposes for the benefit all Americans. The five national forests of New Mexico are sponsors of this program to promote awareness and enjoyment of fish and wildlife on our national forest lands. USDA Forest Service, 517 Gold Avenue, S.W., Albuquerque, NM 87102 (505) 842-3292.

The BUREAU OF LAND MANAGEMENT is responsible for the management of 12.8 million acres of public lands, their resources and values in New Mexico, to best serve the needs of the American people. The goals of multiple-use management is to sustain the integrity, diversity and productivity of ecological systems while providing the goods and services for present and future generations. BLM's Watchable Wildlife program fosters public awareness and appreciation of vast biological, recreational, and educational opportunities offered by America's public lands. For more information, contact the Bureau of Land Management, New Mexico State Office, P. O. Box 27115, Santa Fe, NM 87502 (505) 438-7400.

The U.S. FISH & WILDLIFE SERVICE programs include the national wildlife refuge system, protection of threatened and endangered species, conservation of migratory birds, fisheries restoration, recreation/education, wildlife research, private landowner technical assistance and partnerships, and law enforcement. Help acquire and conserve wildlife refuge habitat by purchasing Federal Duck Stamps. For more information, contact U. S. Fish & Wildlife Service, P. O. Box 1306, Albuquerque, NM 87103 (505) 766-8044.

NEW MEXICO

AMERICA'S LAND
OF ENCHANTMENT

NEW MEXICO DEPARTMENT OF TOURISM creates, promotes, and develops economic benefits to the state through a strong visitor industry that will benefit New Mexico economically, environmentally and culturally. New Mexico Department of Tourism, Lamy Building, 491 Old Santa Fe Trail or P. O. Box 20003, Santa Fe, NM 87503 (505) 827-7400 or (800) 545-2040.

NEW MEXICO HIGHWAY AND TRANSPORTATION DEPARTMENT designs, builds, operates and maintains New Mexico's highway system. It supports Watchable Wildlife by providing special "binoculars" signage at highway and other locations near sites throughout the state. New Mexico Dept. of Highways and Transportation, P. O. Box 1149, Santa Fe, NM 87504 (505) 827-5474.

NEW MEXICO PARK & RECREATION DIVISION manages and conserves New Mexico State Park areas providing opportunities for outdoor recreation. It also acquires, protects, develops and interprets a wide range of natural and cultural resources. Support the park division by purchasing annual passes or become a park volunteer. New Mexico Division of Park & Recreation, Villagra Building, P. O. Box 1147, Santa Fe, NM 87504-1147, (505) 827-7465 or (800) 451-2541 inside New Mexico.

The NATIONAL FISH AND WILDLIFE FOUNDATION, chartered by Congress to stimulate private giving to conservation, is an independent not-for-profit organization. Using federally funded challenge grants, it forges partnerships between the public and private sectors to conserve the nation's fish, wildlife, and plants. National Fish and Wildlife Foundation, 1120 Connecticut Avenue, Washington, D.C. 20036 (202) 857-0166.

The NATIONAL PARK SERVICE manages 335,255.75 acres in New Mexico, including 10 national monuments, two national historical parks, and one national park. The NPS was established to conserve and protect resources unimpaired for future generations while providing for public use and enjoyment. National Park Service, Southwest Regional Office, P. O. Box 728, Santa Fe, NM 87504-0728. (505) 988-6014.

NEW MEXICO
STATE
LAND
OFFICE

The NEW MEXICO STATE LAND OFFICE administers nearly nine million acres of "trust" lands in New Mexico. By law, these lands are managed to produce revenues to support public schools, universities, and other institutions. The State Land Office encourages wildlife viewing on most of its lands, but a recreational access permit must first be obtained. The annual fee is $25 per individual or family. For more information, contact the State Land Office, 310 Old Santa Fe Trail, P. O. Box 1148, Santa Fe, NM 87504, (505) 827-5760.

The DEPARTMENT OF DEFENSE is the steward of about 25 million acres of land in the United States, many of which possess irreplaceable natural and cultural resources. The DoD is pleased to support the Watchable Wildlife program through its Legacy Resource Management Program, a special initiative to enhance the conservation and restoration of natural and cultural resources on military land. For more information, contact the Office of the Deputy Assistant Secretary of Defense (Environment), 400 Army Navy Drive, Suite 206, Arlington, VA 22202-2884.

DEFENDERS OF WILDLIFE is a national, nonprofit organization of more than 80,000 members and supporters dedicated to preserving the natural abundance and diversity of wildlife and its habitat. A one-year membership is $20 and includes six issues of *Defenders*, an award-winning conservation magazine, and *Wildlife Advocate*, an activist-oriented newsletter. To join or for further information, write or call Defenders of Wildlife, 1101 14th Street NW, Suite 1400, Washington, DC 20005, (202) 682-9400.

NEW MEXICO WILDLIFE FOUNDATION is a not-for-profit organization which helps fund wildlife-education projects in New Mexico. For more information, write New Mexico Wildlife Foundation, P. O. Box 22520, Santa Fe, NM 87505 or call Bill Dixon (505) 982-4466.

photo by LA Photo

South of Socorro, the Bosque del Apache National Wildlife Refuge.

Snow geese take wing in the winds of Bosque del Apache.

Every evening, in the pale light of dusk, a remarkable spectacle transforms the autumn skies of New Mexico. As if orchestrated, rare whooping cranes, thousands of snow geese and other magnificent birds take flight in the winds of the Bosque. Here, in the golden marshlands along the Rio Grande, a kingdom of waterfowl takes refuge in the warmth of New Mexico. For more wildlife viewing information on the Bosque, turn to page 68 of this guide. Call 1-800-545-2040, ext. 9426, or write the NM Dept. of Tourism, Rm. 9426, 491 Old Santa Fe Trail, Santa Fe, NM 87503, for a free Vacation Guide.

✴ NEW MEXICO ✴

AMERICA'S LAND OF ENCHANTMENT

THE NATIONAL WATCHABLE WILDLIFE PROGRAM

In 1986, the President's Commission on American Outdoors identified wildlife recreation as one of our nation's most popular outdoor activities. Survey results from a 1991 U. S. Fish & Wildlife Service study showed that "wildlife-related recreation" (not including hunting or fishing) represented a $379 million expenditure in New Mexico alone, up from $364 million in 1985.

For many years, hunters and anglers supplied most of the funding for wildlife conservation through license fees and taxes on firearms and fishing tackle. Today, this revenue base is shrinking and unable to meet future demands. Efforts are under way at state and national levels to develop new funding mechanisms for wildlife conservation and recreation. The national Watchable Wildlife program is one of the catalysts of this new effort.

The national Watchable Wildlife program began in 1990 with the signing of a Memorandum of Understanding among eight federal land management agencies, the International Association of Fish and Wildlife Agencies, and four national conservation groups. Defenders of Wildlife assumed the role of nationwide program coordinator. With many states now implementing the program, Watchable Wildlife will soon be a coast-to-coast network.

In New Mexico, nomination forms for wildlife viewing sites were sent to representatives of participating agencies, chambers of commerce, county extension agents, university science departments, and several others. More than 115 nominations were returned. Representatives from the 13 participating agencies in New Mexico met to review site nominations. Sites were judged on criteria based on likelihood of wildlife to view; reasonable visitor access; scenic beauty; interpretive or access improvements (i.e. barrier-free access); ecological significance; supplemental values; urban wildlife educational opportunity; and whether the site contributed to species diversity for the guidebook. The group finally selected 76 sites for inclusion in this guide.

At this time, not all of these 76 sites are signed or developed. However, plans are underway for a full-time New Mexico Watchable Wildlife Coordinator whose responsibilities will include site enhancement.

All wildlife—both game and non-game, the much-photographed and the seldom-seen—play a role in the continued well-being of Earth's ecosystem. Watchable Wildlife helps expand our understanding of and appreciation for our precious wildlife heritage.

The Watchable Wildlife program works to create an appreciation of the biodiversity in one's own backyard, such as this pronghorn, a familiar species to New Mexicans.
DON L. MacCARTER

TIPS FOR VIEWING WILDLIFE

Much of the excitement of wildlife viewing stems from the fact that you can never be sure of what you will see. While many species are difficult to view under the best of circumstances, there are several things you can do to greatly increase your chances of seeing wild animals in their natural environment.

The cardinal rule of wildlife viewing is patience. You must spend enough time in the field. If you arrive at a viewing site expecting to see every species noted in this guide on your first visit, you will surely be disappointed. Review the tips below, and enjoy your time in the outdoors, regardless of what you see.

Prepare for your outing. Some of the viewing sites in this guide are remote and have no facilities; review each site account before you visit, checking for warnings about services and road conditions. ALWAYS CARRY WATER, EVEN IN WINTER. Dress appropriately for the area and season. Detailed maps of many areas featured in this guide may be obtained through the Forest Service, Bureau of Land Management, or New Mexico State Land Office. Always travel with a current road map.

Visit when animals are active. The first and last hours of daylight are most productive. Early summer evenings can be good for viewing reptiles; in spring and fall, reptiles and amphibians tend to be more active in the warmest period of the day. Many mammals and birds are especially active before or after storms. During summer in desert areas, viewing can be excellent immediately after a rainstorm, or on cloudy days.

Wildlife viewing is often seasonal. Many wildlife species are present only during certain times of year. Waterfowl and shorebirds are best viewed when they migrate through New Mexico in large numbers. Bald eagles may be seen only in certain months. Each site account in this guide contains a wealth of information about optimal seasons for viewing selected species. Consult a field guide for additional information, or call the site owner for an update before you visit.

Use field guides. Pocket field guides are essential for positive identification of the many animals named at each viewing site. Guides are available for virtually every plant and animal found in New Mexico, and contain valuable information about where animals live, what they eat, and when they rear young.

Use binoculars or a spotting scope. Viewing aids will bridge the distance between you and wild animals. Binoculars come in different sizes such as 7x35, 8x40, and 10x50. The first number refers to how large the animal will be magnified compared to the naked eye. A "7x" figure, for example, means that the animal is magnified 7 times larger. The second number in the couplet refers to the diameter of the lens that faces the animal. The larger that number, the greater the amount of light entering the lens—which means better viewing in dim light.

Move slowly and quietly. When you arrive at a viewing site, you can employ several strategies for getting close to wildlife. You can stay in your vehicle and wait for animals to pass by. You can find a comfortable place, sit down, and remain still. Or you can quietly stalk wildlife. Take a few steps, then stop, look, and listen. Use your ears to locate birds or the movements of other animals. Walk into the wind if possible, avoiding brittle sticks or leaves. Use trees and vegetation as a blind. Wear dark-colored clothes or camouflage. Consider using a dropcloth of camouflage netting, or a portable blind.

Enjoy wildlife at a distance. You can actually harm the wildlife you care about by getting too close. Move away from an animal if it stops feeding and raises its head sharply, appears nervous, stands up suddenly, or changes its direction of travel. Causing animals to run or move in winter forces them to use up critical energy reserves needed to survive. Leave your pets at home—they may chase or kill wildlife.

Never touch orphaned or sick animals, especially squirrels or prairie dogs. In New Mexico, squirrels and rodents may carry the bubonic plague or the Hantavirus disease. Young wild animals that appear to be alone usually have parents waiting nearby. If you believe an animal is injured, sick, or abandoned, contact the site owner or the nearest wildlife agency.

Some wildlife can be dangerous. Maintain a safe distance from black bears, especially sows with cubs; rutting bull elk in the fall; and mountain lions and bison bulls at any time of year. Rattlesnakes are active spring through fall, and scorpions are present in summer. Be alert, and view these animals from a safe distance if you encounter them.

Honor the rights of private landowners. A few of the viewing sites in this guide feature roadside wildlife viewing adjacent to private lands. Always get permission before entering private property.

Honor the rights of other wildlife viewers. Keep voices low. If many people are viewing, please be patient and allow others to enjoy a quality experience. Leave wildlife habitat in better condition than you found it. Pick up any litter and dispose of it properly.

PHOTO TIPS

1. For best results with general wildlife photography, use medium-speed films such as ASA (ISO) 100 (Fujichrome or Ektachrome) or ASA (ISO) 64 Kodachrome. For print film, use ASA (ISO) 100 or 200.
2. For landscape/scenic shots, use an ASA (ISO) slower-speed film such as Kodachrome 25, Velvia Fujichrome ASA (ISO) 50, or Ektachrome 50 HC. Kodak's Ektar ASA (ISO) 25 print film is great for enlargements.
3. Early morning and late afternoon are your best times to photograph for two reasons: wildlife is more apt to be active, and the quality of light at that time makes a better picture than the harsh light of midday.
4. Use a wide angle lens (20-28 mm) to capture your scenic shots. Use the greatest depth of field possible.
5. Use a telephoto lens (200-400 mm) for best close-up wildlife shots. It is important that you allow space between you and the animal you're photographing—it allows them to be more natural.
6. Use a tripod to get sharp pictures — you'll be surprised at the results! If you're shooting in dim light (e.g. early-morning/late-evening), consider using a tripod and shutter cable release. This will allow you to use an f-stop

which affords a greater depth of field. Take time to compose your shot.

7. Use a lens hood to help cut glare. It may also help protect your lens in the event you bump it against another object.

8. Do not leave your film and camera in a closed vehicle during hot weather.

HOW TO USE THIS GUIDE

New Mexico is divided into **nine travel regions** shown on the opposite page. **Each region is featured in a separate section** of this book. Each section begins with a **full-page scenic photograph** and **information paragraph** about the area, a **regional map**, and a **site list** for the region. Each region is edged with a special **color bar** for quick access in the guide.

Wildlife **viewing sites are numbered in a general west-to-east pattern.** Each **site name** is preceded by a **site number**. The site **description** gives a brief overview of the habitats and physiographic features found at the site, along with notes on access. It is followed by **wildlife viewing information** including species, chances of viewing, and best times to view. **Directions** to each site are written; supplement these directions with state and/or county road maps. *NOTES OF CAUTION REGARDING ROAD CONDITIONS, VIEWING LIMITA-TIONS, AND OTHER RESTRICTIONS APPEAR IN CAPITAL LETTERS.*

Ownership and Amenities Information—At the end of each site description are the **site owner name(s)** and **phone number(s)** where additional information may be obtained. The name of the **closest town** offering gas and food is listed. **Amenities symbols,** including those for on-site facilities and recreation, are depicted at the end of each description. *Note: please call the site manager for more detailed information about barrier-free access if the symbol appears at that site.*

FACILITIES AND RECREATION SYMBOLS

 Parking

 Restrooms Pit Toilets

 Barrier-free

 Picinic

 Drinking Water

Hiking

 Entry Fee

Camping

Bicycling

 Cross-country Skiing

Horse Trails

Non-Motorized Boats

 Lodging

 Restaurants

 Boat Ramp

 Motorized Boats

NEW MEXICO
Wildlife Viewing Areas

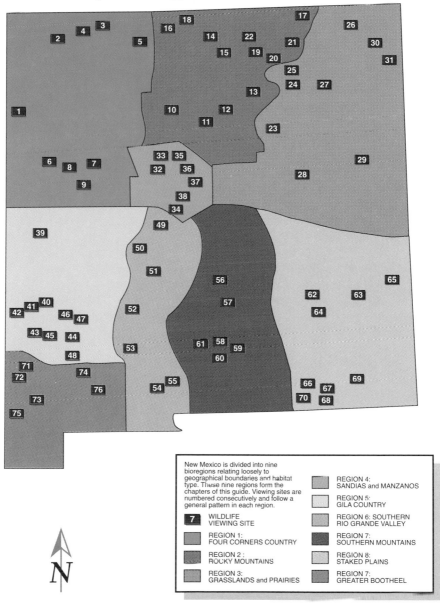

New Mexico is divided into nine bioregions relating loosely to geographical boundaries and habitat type. These nine regions form the chapters of this guide. Viewing sites are numbered consecutively and follow a general pattern in each region.

7 WILDLIFE VIEWING SITE

REGION 1: FOUR CORNERS COUNTRY

REGION 2: ROCKY MOUNTAINS

REGION 3: GRASSLANDS and PRAIRIES

REGION 4: SANDIAS and MANZANOS

REGION 5: GILA COUNTRY

REGION 6: SOUTHERN RIO GRANDE VALLEY

REGION 7: SOUTHERN MOUNTAINS

REGION 8: STAKED PLAINS

REGION 7: GREATER BOOTHEEL

HIGHWAY SIGNS

As you travel in New Mexico and other states, look for these special highway signs that identify wildlife viewing sites. These signs will help guide you to the viewing area. NOTE: Be sure to read the written directions provided with each site in this book — highway signs may refer to more than one site along a particular route.

13

WHERE TO WATCH WILDLIFE IN NEW MEXICO

Known to visitors as The Land of Enchantment, New Mexico is also a land of contrasts. Six of the West's seven life zones are found here. Each life zone is a unique combination of elevation and climatic conditions that create distinct habitats for wildlife. The distribution of New Mexico's six life zones is shown on the opposite page.

1. **Alpine Zone (11,500 feet).** This zone includes the windswept tundra above tree line. Look for this zone in the higher reaches of the Pecos and Wheeler Peak wilderness areas, and on the very top of Sierra Blanca, a volcanic peak near Ruidoso.

2. **Subalpine Zone (9,500 feet).** Also called the Hudsonian Zone, this area includes forests of Englemann spruce, subalpine fir, corkbark fir, bristlecone pine, and other species. Some of the mountain ranges containing this life zone are the Jemez, Sandia, Sacramento, Mount Taylor, and the Sangre de Cristo.

3. **Mixed Coniferous Zone (8,500 feet).** Also called the Canadian Life Zone, this area includes forests of Douglas-fir, white fir, aspen, and occasional ponderosa pine. Some examples of viewing sites located in this zone are the Sargent Wildlife Area, and the Mogollon Road in Gila Country.

4. **Transition Zone (7,000 feet).** Also called the Mountain Zone, Ponderosa pines predominate in this life zone. Examples of some viewing sites located in this zone include Lake Roberts and Rice Park.

5. **Upper Sonoran Life Zone (4,500 feet).** Also called the Grasslands/Woodlands Zone, this largest life zone in New Mexico generally consists of piñon pine, juniper species, scrub oak, and grasses. Some examples of viewing sites located in this zone are the Wild Rivers Recreation Area, the Kiowa Grasslands, Mescalero Sands, Capulin Volcano, and along the Road to the Gila Cliff Dwellings at the high mesa.

6. **Lower Sonoran Life Zone (3,000 feet).** This is a desert region. In southern New Mexico, the desert plants found there are designated as belonging to the Chihuahuan Desert. Examples of viewing sites located in this zone include Granite Gap, Oliver Lee State Park, Aguirre Spring, the Red Rock Wildlife Area and others.

New Mexico Life Zones

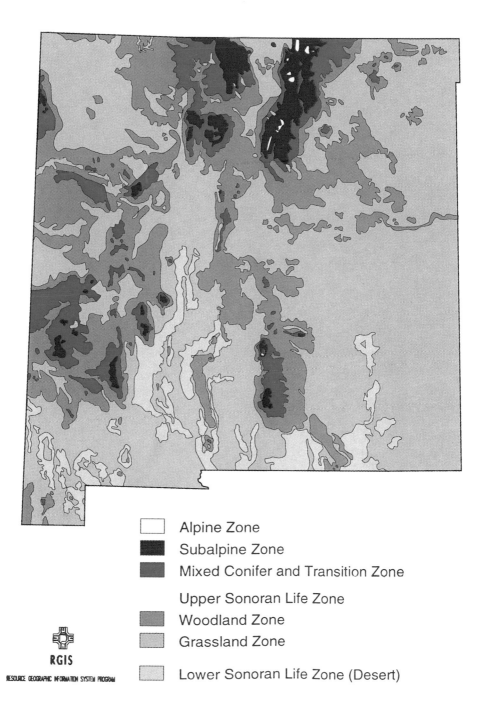

Alpine Zone
Subalpine Zone
Mixed Conifer and Transition Zone

Upper Sonoran Life Zone
Woodland Zone
Grassland Zone

Lower Sonoran Life Zone (Desert)

RGIS
RESOURCE GEOGRAPHIC INFORMATION SYSTEM PROGRAM

Biodiversity in New Mexico

Sandhill crane

Mountain lion

Kangaroo rat

Largemouth bass

Blue-winged teal

Rio Grande cutthroat trout

Spadefoot toad

Desert bighorn sheep

White-tailed ptarmigan

Lesser prairie chicken

Black-chinned hummingbird

Texas horned toad

Greater roadrunner

Javelina (collared peccary)

Move quietly, look carefully, and you will discover a rich world of wildlife, great and small, in New Mexico: 145 species of mammals, 92 reptiles, 26 amphibians, 120 fish, and 485 species of birds. The term "biodiversity" refers to all life forms, plants as well as animals, that function together to form earth's ecosystems. Each plant and animal plays a role in sustaining the natural balance of life, keeping nature alive, healthy, and self-perpetuating.

Worth Watching, Worth Conserving

Kit fox

Abert squirrel

Monarch butterfly

American avocet

Western painted turtle

Black-tailed jackrabbit

Rocky Mountain elk

Piñon jay

Damsel fly

Black-tailed prairie dog

Collared lizard

Black-tailed rattlesnake

Yellow-headed blackbird

With each extinction, nature loses more of what it needs to function best: diversity of life. Biodiversity is important because it enables nature's systems to work smoothly. Biodiversity also provides enjoyment when we go out to observe wildlife and experience nature. Each species is unique, a product of millions of years of evolution. Each species, and humankind, too, depends on every other species for its continued survival and well-being.

REGION 1: FOUR CORNERS COUNTRY

Four state boundaries—New Mexico, Colorado, Utah, and Arizona—join at a single point at Four Corners, the only place in the U.S. where this occurs. In this region, part of the West's Great Basin, large numbers of Canada geese may be seen along the San Juan River. Migrating bald eagles are abundant along the San Juan and La Plata rivers, as well as Navajo Reservoir during the winter months. Deer and elk are locally abundant in many areas. Four Corners Country is also known for its intriguing rock formations, including Shiprock (facing page), a sacred place to the Navajo people.

Photo, opposite page: Shiprock. **GARY RASMUSSEN**

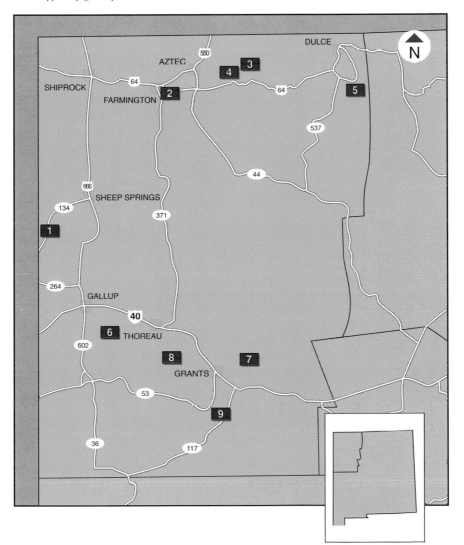

Wildlife Viewing Sites

1. Chuska Mountains to Red Lake	5. Jicarilla Lakes Loop
2. River Reach Terrace, Berg Park	6. Rice Park
3. Navajo Lake State Park: San Juan River Unit	7. Mount Taylor Road
	8. Zuni Mountains Tour
4. Simon Canyon, Cottonwood Campground	9. El Malpais National Monument and National Conservation Area

1 CHUSKA MOUNTAINS TO RED LAKE

Description: *AUTO TOUR.* This drive on Navajo Nation land crosses the picturesque Chuska Mountains en route to Red Lake Waterfowl Management Area. A stopping place for migratory waterfowl, Red Lake is rimmed by bulrushes and set against a backdrop of low forested hills and red sandstone cliffs. Restrooms and picnic area on Narbona Pass; no facilities at Red Lake. Round-trip drive is 30 miles; total driving time is approximately 45 minutes.

Viewing Information: Possible sightings of bald eagles during migration, November through December and February through March. Good viewing of red-winged blackbird, great blue heron, northern harrier, and red-tailed hawk. Ruddy ducks, mallards, redheads, Canada geese, and eared grebes abundant during breeding season.

Directions: *From Shiprock, drive south on U.S. Highway 666 or travel north from Gallup, about 47 miles either way. Turn west at Sheep Springs on New Mexico Highway 134. The road climbs to Narbona Pass. Continue 10 miles past Narbona Pass Campground to the junction with BIA Highway 12. Turn left at the sign for Navajo and drive 6 miles. The road follows the lake shore to its southern tip—a dirt road to the right provides access. Make another immediate right across the cattleguard and continue 0.5 mile to the lake. LAST HALF-MILE OF ROAD IMPASSABLE IN WET WEATHER.*

Closest Town: Navajo, New Mexico

Ownership: Navajo Nation Fish and Wildlife (602) 871-7068　

2 RIVER REACH TERRACE, BERG PARK

Description: This 2-mile-long urban park in a natural *bosque* (riverside woodlands) along the Animas River offers a series of woodland and riverside hiking trails. This is a project of the River Reach Foundation and the City of Farmington to preserve one of the last remaining cottonwood groves along the Animas River.

Viewing Information: Occasional viewing of rock squirrel, muskrat, beaver, raccoon, porcupine, black-billed magpie, and Canada geese year-round, as well as migratory waterfowl October through March. Look for western painted turtles. Mule deer may be seen year-round; bald eagles are present November through March. Other birds here include the yellow-breasted chat, blue grosbeak, rufous-sided towhee, northern oriole, great blue heron, long-eared owl, ring-necked pheasant, and screech owl.

Directions: *Three access points in Farmington. Turn on Scott Avenue off U.S. Highway 550 at "T" intersection. Turn left 100 yards past first light, watch for sign marking entrance. Another access is via San Juan Boulevard onto Fairview Avenue. The third access is from Animas Park, south of the river off Browning Parkway.*

Closest Town: Farmington

Ownership: City of Farmington, (505) 599-1181　

Description: This scenic stretch of the San Juan River, known locally as the Texas Hole, is New Mexico's premier trout fishery. Here the river flows through a sandstone canyon with piñon/juniper mesas on either side. February is the best month for viewing, as the area greens up, visitor numbers are still low, and biting insects are at a minimum. Mule deer frequent the area at this time. Visit just before dawn, mid-week, to avoid groups of anglers.

Viewing Information: Rainbow, brown and hybrid cutthroat-rainbow trout may be seen year-round. During insect hatches, trout congregate in groups (known to anglers as "pods") to feed, and may be seen in large numbers—watch for small dimples and rings on the surface of the river, created when a fish tips upward to take an insect. Five barrier-free ramps provide good viewing. Canada geese have begun nesting in recent years on rocks above the river and may be seen year-round. Good winter viewing of bald eagles, and such waterfowl as mallard, common merganser, common goldeneye, gadwall, American wigeon, bufflehead, and cinnamon and blue-winged teal. Beaver and muskrat also present.

Directions: *From Aztec, go east on U.S. Highway 550 for 1 mile and turn right onto New Mexico Highway 173 at sign for Navajo Dam State Park. Continue about 19 miles and turn left at the "T" junction with NM 511. Continue east another 2 miles and turn left at the paved road near the little adobe Catholic church and go 0.5 mile to the river.*

Closest Town: Aztec

Ownership: New Mexico Park & Recreation Division; Navajo Lake State Park, San Juan River Unit (505) 632-1770

The San Juan River, where it passes through Navajo Lake State Park, offers good viewing of wild trout. DENVER BRYAN

4 | SIMON CANYON, COTTONWOOD CAMPGROUND

Description: Two neighboring areas provide visitors with different aspects of the same cottonwood riverside habitat. Cottonwood Campground is park-like, with green grass, mostly paved access, and many amenities, while Simon Canyon is more remote, allows backpacking and horses, and offers a hiking trail to a Navajo rock shelter dating from the early 1700s. Tent camping only at Simon Canyon; no wood fires permitted. Day-use fee at Cottonwood Campground.

Viewing Information: Along the river at both sites, look for downed trees, chew marks, and other evidence of beaver activity. Occasional viewing of muskrat, rock squirrel, weasel, porcupine, and raccoon. Good viewing of bald eagles November through March, as well as oriole, piñon jay, cliff and violet-green swallow, black-billed magpie, northern flicker, flycatcher, and several species of woodpecker. Year-round viewing of Canada geese, which often nest here. Waterfowl may be seen April through June, and mid-October through early December—watch for northern pintail, bufflehead, mallard, and cinnamon teal. Deer frequently use Simon Canyon as a fawning area April through June. The canyon offers good viewing of diverse bird species: white-throated swift, canyon wren, mourning dove, and raptors, including turkey vulture, sharp-shinned hawk, American kestrel, northern harrier, golden eagle, and red-tailed hawk. Rare sightings of peregrine falcon. After the spring runoff, watch for rainbow, brown and hybrid cutthroat-rainbow trout in the clear waters of the San Juan River.

Directions: *From Aztec, drive northeast on U.S. Highway 550 for 1 mile, and turn right onto New Mexico Highway 173 at sign for Navajo Dam State Park. Continue 18 miles to Cottonwood Campground entrance on left. To reach Simon Canyon, continue 3.7 miles past campground.*

Closest Town: Aztec

Ownership: Cottonwood Campground, New Mexico Park & Recreation Division (505) 632-1770; Simon Canyon Recreation Area, Bureau of Land Management (505) 327-5344

Weighing up to 50 lbs., the beaver is an exclusive vegetarian, dependent on permanent bodies of water in order to survive.
DON L. MacCARTER

Description: *AUTO TOUR.* This driving loop of 52 miles passes through forested hills to five lakes managed by the Jicarilla Apache Tribe. The largest, Burford Lake, known locally as Stinking Lake because of its abundant algae, is a 1,300-acre marsh surrounded by sagebrush flats—the largest natural lake in New Mexico. The other four lakes are easily accessible, most from paved roads. October is a good time to visit, when Gambel oaks change to flaming scarlet amidst the pine and sage. No facilities along route.

Viewing Information: Excellent viewing of Canada geese and other migratory waterfowl during fall migration, October and November, with fair viewing in April. Lakes freeze over December - February. Very good viewing of such wading birds as the American avocet, black-crowned night heron, and white-faced ibis, May through September. Also watch at this time for yellow-headed blackbird, eared grebe, marsh wren, vesper sparrow, and cinnamon teal. Look for the plains spadefoot toad. Very good viewing of bald eagles November through February, and golden eagles year-round. Occasional viewing of elk, mule deer, coyote, wild turkey, and long-tailed weasel. Peregrine falcon and black bear rarely seen. *ANY ACTIVITY OTHER THAN WILDLIFE VIEWING IN OR NEAR A VEHICLE REQUIRES A TRIBAL PERMIT.*

Directions: *See map at right. Traveling west from Dulce, turn left (south) onto Highway J-8 at the Conoco station. Continue 17 miles to west shore of Stone Lake. Drive south past Stone Lake on J-8 and continue 7 miles on gravel road to Burford Lake. Then backtrack to Stone Lake and junction of J-8 and J-15. Turn left (west) onto J-15 and drive 7 miles to New Mexico Highway 537, and turn right. After 1 mile, take first right to drive along shore of La Jara Lake. Then return to NM 537 and turn right. Continue 9 miles back to Dulce.*

Closest Town: Dulce

Ownership: Jicarilla Game and Fish

(505) 759-3255

Nicknamed 'Baldpate,' the American Wigeon, classified as a puddle duck, is commonly seen throughout New Mexico during fall and winter months.
MIKE PELLEGATTI

6 RICE PARK

Description: This small reservoir—also known as Rice Lake—is situated in a shallow bowl on a high mountain mesa in the Cibola National Forest. Young ponderosa pines grow closely about the shores of this lake, which is managed as waterfowl habitat. Water levels fluctuate seasonally and range from high to nearly dry. Reservoir gates are usually opened in late May or early June to drain waters; however, there is nearly always a 1- to 3-acre pool, even in dry years. No facilities on site.

Viewing Information: Lake access road is open April through September only. During this time, view migratory waterfowl, including mallard, northern pintail, green-winged and cinnamon teal, wigeon, gadwall, lesser scaup, and occasional Canada geese—best viewing in April and May. Watch for elk, especially at dawn and dusk in September; frequent tracks and sign. Spring and summer birds include the Steller's jay, white-breasted and pygmy nuthatch, pine siskin, vesper sparrow, robin, red-tailed hawk, northern harrier, and swallow species, including violet-green, cliff, and barn.

Directions: *Exit Interstate 40 at Thoreau. Turn left on frontage road. Go under the highway onto paved New Mexico Highway 612. Drive 9 miles, then turn right onto gravel Forest Road 569 and cross cattleguard. Continue 8 miles to gated access at right; gate has 2 red signs at each end. Park on side of the road; walk 0.5 mile to lake, clearly visible from the road.*

Closest Town: Thoreau

Ownership: USDA Forest Service (505) 287-8833

Common in conifer and pine-oak forests of the Rocky Mountains, the Steller's Jay often mimics the cry of the golden eagle or the red-tailed hawk.
DON L. MacCARTER

7 MOUNT TAYLOR ROAD

Description: *AUTO TOUR.* This drive traverses 11,301-foot Mount Taylor, a northwest New Mexico landmark. The road passes through piñon- and juniper-covered hills and meadows, Gambel oak and ponderosa pine, culminating in subalpine aspen, spruce, and fir woodlands. The round-trip tour, from Grants to La Mosca Saddle and back, is 46 miles. *ROAD OPEN JUNE - OCTOBER, IMPASSABLE IN WET WEATHER. BRING WATER.*

Viewing Information: At milepost 8, look into the meadows on both sides of the road for elk, especially at dawn and dusk. Wild turkey are common in this area, as well as black bear and mule deer. At La Mosca Saddle, watch for elk in the meadow and raptors soaring overhead. Other birds include the band-tailed pigeon, pine siskin, Steller's jay, Clark's nutcracker, and nuthatch species.

Directions: *Take New Mexico Highway 547 (paved Lobo Canyon Road) northeast from Grants. Pavement ends at milepost 13 and gravel Forest Road 239 begins at this point. Continue 3 miles and turn right onto Forest Road 453 to the La Mosca fire tower lookout. The well-maintained gravel road becomes extremely rough at this point. Take right fork another 2 miles to La Mosca Saddle.*

Closest Town: Grants

Ownership: USDA Forest Service (505) 287-8833

The omnivorous black bear frequently overturns stumps or rocks in search of grubs and insects. DON L. MacCARTER

8 ZUNI MOUNTAINS TOUR

Description: *AUTO TOUR.* In the Zuni Mountains, layers of alternating sandstone and shale have eroded over time into today's picturesque countryside. This 50-mile tour begins in the town of Thoreau, passes through the narrow canyons, ponderosa pine forests, and cottonwood riparian zones of the Zuni Mountains, and ends in the town of Grants.

Viewing Information: Look for a beaver dam 0.5 mile west of Bluewater Creek Picnic Area. Early-morning birding in cottonwood bottoms along the hiking trail may yield sightings of nuthatches and jays, pine siskin, and red crossbill. Along the route at Ojo Redondo Campground, look for wild turkey, red-tailed hawk, and Abert squirrel. Occasional viewing of mule deer, elk, and black bear at the campground.

Directions: *Also see map at right. Exit Interstate 40 at Thoreau. Drive south on New Mexico Highway 612. Continue about 3 miles past the entrance to Bluewater Lake State Park; here the pavement ends and road becomes gravel Forest Road 178. After about 2 miles, watch for beaver dam on left. Continue 0.5 mile to the Bluewater Creek Picnic and Hiking Trail. Continue south on FR 178, and turn left at FR 480 (Post Office Flats). Drive 3 miles to reach Ojo Redondo Campground. Continue about 9 miles to junction of FR 49; turn left and follow Zuni Canyon 10 miles into Grants.*

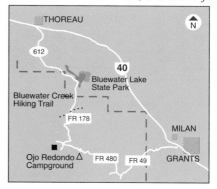

Closest Town: Grants

Ownership: USDA Forest Service (505) 287-8833

Abert squirrels are widespread in the ponderosa pine forests of New Mexico. These squirrels take shelter in the pines and rely heavily upon them for food.
DON L. MacCARTER

Description: This vast area of volcanic and sandstone formations encompasses a broad valley with 30 cinder cones bounding it on the west, sandstone rimrock to the east, and dry plains to the south. Stop at 1 of 2 visitor centers, in Grants or on New Mexico Highway 117, for maps and additional information.

Viewing Information: Much of the national monument and conservation area are wilderness, with opportunities for viewing diverse wildlife. The sandstone rimrock country is home to black bear, mule deer, coyote, prairie dog, bobcat, and burrowing owl. The red-tailed hawk, American kestrel, and turkey vulture soar overhead, while violet-green swallow and canyon wren are commonly seen closer to the cliffs. Peregrine falcons have been sighted. More than two dozen bison were transplanted here in 1992, and pronghorn abound on the southern rangeland areas. Lava flows provide habitat for diverse species, including various reptiles, woodrats, and mice. These creatures exhibit a melanistic adaptation which causes darker colors in their coats and skins, making them harder to see.

Directions: *Two paved state highways, New Mexico 53 on the west side and NM 117 on the east side, provide access off Interstate 40.*

Closest Town: Grants

Ownership: National Park Service, El Malpais National Monument (505) 285-4641; Bureau of Land Management, El Malpais National Conservation Area (505) 285-5406

El Malpais, the "Bad Land," is home to diverse species, some of which exhibit melanistic coloring to blend in with the surrounding terrain. MARK NOHL/NM MAGAZINE

REGION 2: ROCKY MOUNTAINS

The southernmost portion of the Rocky Mountain chain ends in foothills just south of Santa Fe, in northern New Mexico. Several wilderness areas are located in this region, as well as the Jemez and Sangre de Cristo mountain ranges. Variations in elevation have created four life zones in this region: alpine, subalpine, mixed coniferous, and transition zones (for more on life zones, see page 15). This area is typified by aspen parklands and spruce-fir forests, where such wildlife as blue grouse, Rocky Mountain elk, mountain lion, black bear, and snowshoe hare can be found.

Photo, opposite page: Santa Fe Baldy. DON L. MacCARTER

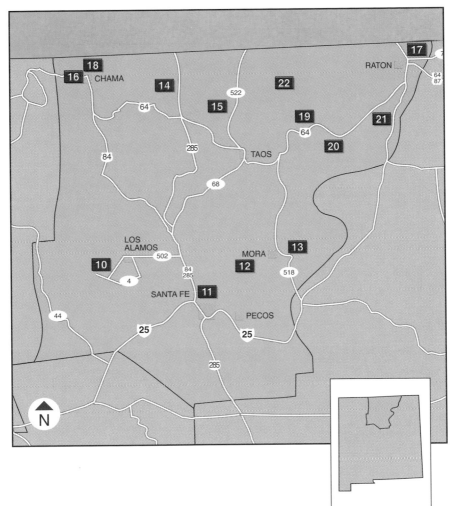

Wildlife Viewing Sites

10.	Valle Grande		
11.	Randall Davey Audubon Center	17.	Sugarite Canyon State Park
12	Pecos Wilderness	18.	Edward Sargent Wildlife
13.	Salman Ranch		Management Area
14.	San Antonio Mountain, Stewart	19.	Cimarron Canyon
	Meadows	20.	Philmont Ranch Road
15.	Wild Rivers Recreation Area	21.	Maxwell National Wildlife Refuge
16.	W.A. "Bill" Humphries Wildlife Area	22.	Valle Vidal Unit

10 VALLE GRANDE

Description: Many elk graze in Valle Grande, a broad, volcanic caldera ringed by forested mountains. Two major eruptions, estimated at one million and 1.4 million years ago, created the caldera. The last eruption in the Jemez Range occurred about 140,000 years ago. The mountain used to be the largest peak in this region until its apex collapsed, creating the grassy bowl seen today. The *valle* is now part of a private ranch.

Viewing Information: Binoculars or a spotting scope are essential here for viewing a sizeable elk herd that can include 250 animals at a time. Best viewing is between 6 p.m. and nightfall during the summer. Listen for bull elk bugling on October evenings. Cattle may also graze near the elk herds. *VALLE GRANDE IS PRIVATE PROPERTY. PLEASE RESPECT LANDOWNER'S RIGHTS—VIEW FROM ROADSIDE ONLY.*

Directions: *At the Los Alamos National Laboratory complex, travel through 4 stoplights and continue straight toward the mountains on New Mexico Highway 502/501, the road that runs in front of the laboratory; do not take the immediate right fork. At 4.3 miles, where road comes to a "T", turn right onto NM 4. The paved road climbs sharply through a series of switchbacks. At 12.5 miles, watch for 3 pull-outs on right overlooking Valle Grande.*

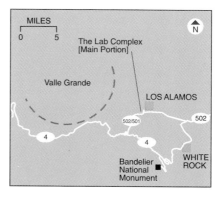

Closest Town: Los Alamos

Ownership: Land privately owned.

Elk were extirpated in New Mexico during the early 1900s. They were reintroduced shortly after, and elk are now found in most mountainous areas of the state.
DON L. MacCARTER

Description: Built as a sawmill in 1847, the tree-shaded former home of early 20th-century artist Randall Davey is now the Randall Davey Audubon Center in Santa Fe. This historic site in the foothills of the Sangre de Cristo mountains affords good wildlife viewing close to Santa Fe. Hilly piñon-juniper woodlands and meadows climb to an area of ponderosa pine forest, typical habitat types for northern New Mexico at 7,500 feet. Various activities are offered at the center, including nature hikes, wildlife interpretive programs, and scheduled tours of the mansion.

Viewing Information: More than 140 species of birds are seen here seasonally, along with abundant sign of coyote, fox, and raccoon. Occasional sightings of black bear in fall. Raptors and waterfowl are present during fall migration. Look for the many-lined skink and smooth green snake, both common in the area. Songbirds abundant year-round.

Directions: In Santa Fe, take paved Upper Canyon Road (it begins across from Cristo Rey Church on the east side of downtown). Take the road all the way to its end, about 2 miles. The last 0.5 mile of the road is dirt and often muddy in spring.

Closest Town: Santa Fe

Ownership: National Audubon Society (505) 983-4609

The handsome rufous-sided towhee is easy to identify with its black, white, and rust-colored feathers, and reddish-colored eyes. LARRY BROCK

12 ▌PECOS WILDERNESS

Description: This vast, spectacular high-mountain wilderness includes 15 lakes and 30 perennial streams, with elevations ranging from 8,400 to 13,103 feet. The mountains are forested with Engelmann spruce, corkbark fir, ponderosa pine, Douglas-fir, white fir, limber pine, bristlecone pine, and aspen. Abundant wildflowers in spring and summer. There are 34 entry points into wilderness; visitors must hike at least 6 miles in from all trailheads. Stop at the Pecos - Las Vegas Ranger District office for maps and access information; office is open weekdays 9 a.m. to 4:30 p.m. Directions to office appear below.

Viewing Information: Very good chance of seeing Rocky Mountain bighorn sheep near Pecos Baldy, Jose Vigal, and Truchas lakes. Look for white-tailed ptarmigan at Jicarita Peak, Truchas Lakes, and Chimayosas Peak from June 15 through September 1, depending on snowpack. Good viewing of elk, with occasional golden eagles December 15 through April 1, on south-facing slope of Round Mountain adjacent to Jack's Creek Campground—to reach this area, follow New Mexico Highway 63 to locked gate at Cowles and continue on foot or horseback. Entire area offers good to excellent summer viewing of mule deer, yellow-bellied marmot, pika, blue grouse, Abert squirrel, long-tailed weasel, ermine, red squirrel, Clark's nutcracker, and hermit thrush. Rare summer sightings of black bear and wild turkey. Expect dry weather May and June; afternoon rainstorms common July and August.

Directions: *To reach ranger station, take the Pecos exit off Interstate 25, just east of Santa Fe, onto New Mexico Highway 50. Travel 5 miles into Pecos and turn right onto NM 63. Drive 3 blocks to ranger station on right. One easy wilderness access is located north of the village of Pecos, past Terrero, to the trailhead and horse corrals at Jack's Creek and Iron Gate campgrounds.*

Closest Town: Pecos

Ownership: USDA Forest Service (505) 757-6121

The male blue grouse engorges purplish neck sacs and yellow-orange eye 'combs' as part of his courtship display.
BOB BAVIN

13 ▪ SALMAN RANCH

Description: The picturesque Salman Ranch, designated a national historic site, also offers excellent viewing of migratory waterfowl at La Cueva Waterfowl Refuge. An old gristmill, the San Rafael Church, and many other adobe and rock structures testify to this area's interesting history.

Viewing Information: Excellent viewing of Canada geese and other waterfowl in October and November; some geese nest here in summer. Wintering bald eagles may be seen November through February. Very good viewing of broad-tailed and black-chinned hummingbird, common yellowthroat, red-winged blackbird, and swallow species during spring and summer. Occasional dawn/dusk viewing of elk as they venture down from the hills to feed on alfalfa. Also watch for Gunnison's prairie dog, pronghorn, and rarely-seen bison. Most popular visiting time is when the ranch-grown raspberries go on sale, late August through early October.

Directions: Travel north of Las Vegas on New Mexico Highway 518 for 25 miles. Turn right onto NM 442 and continue to ranch. About 100 yards past the ranch store, turn right at the old pine tree near the nursery sign. Follow dirt road to the three forks; take left fork to reach lakes.

Closest Town: Mora

Ownership: Salman Ranch (505) 387-2900

14 ▪ SAN ANTONIO MOUNTAIN, STEWART MEADOWS

Description: An important big game wintering area, San Antonio Mountain rises 10,908 feet from a sagebrush plain. It is home to elk, mule deer, and pronghorn populations. Along its southern perimeter, Stewart Meadows marsh attracts waterfowl and wading birds, including sandhill cranes.

Viewing Information: Viewing **at San Antonio Mountain** is from roadside pullouts only; binoculars or a spotting scope are highly recommended. Excellent viewing for mule deer, elk, and pronghorn late November through March. Also watch for white-tailed jackrabbit in the big sage areas. **At Stewart Meadows**, look for mallard, American wigeon, northern pintail, sandhill crane, common yellowthroat, and sora in the fall; a few species remain year-round.

Directions: From the flashing yellow light in Tres Piedras, drive 11 miles north on U.S. Highway 285 to Forest Road 87 and the sign for Stewart Meadows Waterfowl Area. Turn left and continue 8 miles—meadows are down the hill on right. Back on U.S. 285, travel north 19 miles to the first San Antonio Mountain sign.

Closest Town: Tres Piedras

Ownership: Bureau of Land Management (505) 758-8851; USDA Forest Service (505) 758-8678; New Mexico Department of Game and Fish (505) 445-2311; New Mexico State Land Office (505) 827-5033

15 | WILD RIVERS RECREATION AREA

Description: Two nationally-designated wild and scenic rivers, the Red and Rio Grande, converge at this site and rush through a rugged gorge more than 800 feet deep. Lush grasses, piñon/juniper, and sagebrush surround the gorge. A small driving loop offers good wildlife viewing. La Junta Overlook offers a spectacular view; five of the area's many hiking trails lead to the bottom of the gorge. Bring water.

Viewing Information: Very good year-round viewing of mule deer and elk at dawn/dusk in the loop area; elk are best seen in late winter during pre-dawn hours. Coyote and a variety of birds may be viewed in summer at any time of day—watch for the black-billed magpie, turkey vulture, common raven, scrub jay, northern flicker, and hairy and downy woodpecker. Little brown bats appear on summer evenings. Look for the Gunnison's prairie dog village near the sign for La Junta Overlook. Good year-round viewing of golden eagle and red-tailed hawk. Bald eagles use the river corridor in winter; ducks and geese occur along both rivers in summer. The western tanager, violet-green swallow, Clark's nutcracker, and white-throated swift are present spring through fall. Many broad-tailed hummingbirds nest here in May, and stay through October. Abundant mountain bluebirds. Evenings, watch for elusive ringtails at the bottom of the gorge near the shelters. Spring and fall wildflowers. Weekend guided hikes in summer.

Directions: *From the stoplight in Questa, travel north 2.6 miles on New Mexico Highway 522. Follow signs to entrance. Visitor center is 5.4 miles from entrance.*

Closest Town: Questa

Ownership: Bureau of Land Management, (505) 758-8851; New Mexico State Land Office, (505) 827-5033

Evenings, watch for the elusive ringtail at the bottom of the gorge near the shelters.
DON L. MacCARTER

16 | W. A. "BILL" HUMPHRIES WILDLIFE AREA

Description: This 10-mile dirt track through forested hills and meadows of thick grass provides a good site from which mountain bikers, hikers, and horseback riders can watch for wildlife. No motorized vehicles are permitted on site; bicycle travel is allowed on the main road only. A locked gate two-thirds of the way around the track marks the boundary of private property.

Viewing Information: Excellent evening viewing of elk, with best dates July 1 through mid-September. Black bear and mountain lion are present though rarely seen. Summer viewing of American kestrel, black-billed magpie, mountain bluebird, warblers, band-tailed pigeon, wild turkey, and waterfowl. Western chorus frog and mule deer in summer. Watch for northern shrike November through March. *SITE CLOSES MAY 15 THROUGH JULY 1 FOR ELK CALVING SEASON, AS WELL AS 2 WEEKS PRIOR TO THE START OF ELK HUNTING SEASON AND CLOSED BETWEEN HUNTS. WILDLIFE VIEWING NOT RECOMMENDED DURING ELK HUNTS, OCTOBER - DECEMBER. CONTACT SITE MANAGER FOR SPECIFIC DATES.*

Directions: *At the south edge of Chama, turn left onto U.S. Highway 84/64. Continue west 8 miles to the "Bill" Humphries Wildlife Area, 1 mile past the Continental Divide sign on the south side of the highway. Access is provided through a small wire gate next to locked iron gate. After reaching gate to private property, backtrack for a total distance of 16 miles.*

Closest Town: Chama

Ownership: New Mexico Dept. of Game and Fish
(505) 756-2585 or 841-8881

17 | SUGARITE CANYON STATE PARK

Description: Three reservoir lakes lie along perennial Chicorica Creek between 2 mesas in scenic Sugarite Canyon. Along with conifers, the park contains many deciduous trees, such as New Mexico locust and Gambel oak. Visit mid-week in summer for best viewing; crowds on weekends and holidays.

Viewing Information: Excellent viewing of Abert squirrel and wild turkey year-round. Seasonal viewing of yellow-bellied marmot. Good viewing of mule deer, with occasional viewing of beaver. Elk, black bear, mountain lion, and bobcat present, but not easily observed. Watch for migratory waterfowl on the lakes September through November. Other wildlife includes red-tailed hawk, green-tailed and rufous-sided towhee, northern flicker, mountain and western bluebird, turkey vulture, muskrat, coyote, and gray fox.

Directions: *At Raton, take Interstate 25 exit 452 to New Mexico Highway 72. Travel east about 7 miles to the junction of NM 526. Take the left fork, which goes uphill; continue on to the visitors center and beyond to access the lakes. Improved gravel road leads to Soda Pocket Campground.*

Closest Town: Raton

Ownership: New Mexico Park and
Recreation Division, (505) 445-5607

18 EDWARD SARGENT WILDLIFE MANAGEMENT AREA

Description: The edges of this lush basin rise up to meet thickly forested hills and rugged Chama Peak. A small trout stream, the Rio Chamita, flows through the site. Follow the level dirt road on foot, horseback, or mountain bike about 10 miles to the Colorado border, or turn right onto a graded dirt road—about 3.5 miles from the entrance—that leads to Nabor Lake, a small reservoir. Keep to the left as the road forks. Closed to all vehicle travel. Visitors should bring water.

Viewing Information: Excellent dawn/dusk viewing of elk, with best viewing dates July 1 through mid-September. Frequent glimpses of mule deer, coyote, porcupine, and black bear; resident mountain lion and snowshoe hare are rarely seen. Common summer birds include the American kestrel, mountain bluebird, broad-tailed and black-chinned hummingbird, northern flicker, Steller's jay, Clark's nutcracker, mountain chickadee, brown creeper, warbling vireo, common nighthawk, red-winged blackbird, and northern shrike. Occasional wild turkey or blue grouse. Look for beaver sign and western chorus frogs at Nabor Lake and along the Rio Chamita. *SITE CLOSES TO ALL ACCESS MAY 15 THROUGH JULY 1 FOR ELK CALVING SEASON. AREA IS ALSO CLOSED 2 WEEKS PRIOR TO THE START OF ELK SEASON AND CLOSED BETWEEN ALL ELK HUNTS. WILDLIFE VIEWING NOT RECOMMENDED DURING ELK HUNTS, OCTOBER - DECEMBER. CALL SITE MANAGER FOR DATES.*

Directions: *At the north end of Chama, turn left onto First Street at the Chama Medical Clinic sign. Go 1 block, then turn right on Pine Avenue, which becomes gravel after 1 mile. After 200 yards, watch for 2 iron gates. If first iron gate is locked, the area is closed to all access; second gate down the road remains locked year-round. There is horse and bike access to the left of the gate.*

Closest Town: Chama

Ownership: New Mexico Dept. of Game and Fish (505) 756-2585 or 841-8881

Mule deer are most active at dawn and dusk, when they can be seen at this site browsing on twigs and shrubs.
DON L. MacCARTER

19 | CIMARRON CANYON

Description: This site includes Cimarron Canyon State Park, located within the 33,000-acre Colin Neblett Wildlife Area. The swiftly-flowing Cimarron River traverses its namesake canyon, while the Tolby Meadows Trail climbs to wooded mountains of the wildlife area. The Palisades Picnic Area of the state park features rugged cliffs of monzonite, a volcanic rock, which tower 800 feet. Park offers various pullouts, camping, and picnic areas. At least one person per group must have a valid New Mexico hunting or fishing license in order to camp at the state park.

Viewing Information: Wildlife may be viewed early mornings and late evenings along the Cimarron River and the adjacent wildlife area. Hiking to more remote locales on surrounding mesas and mountains offers a better chance for good viewing of elk, mule deer, and wild turkey year-round, and an occasional black bear. Excellent year-round viewing of Abert squirrel, golden-mantled ground squirrel, and Colorado and least chipmunk.

Directions: *From Eagle Nest, travel 3 miles east on U.S. Highway 64 to park/ wildlife area signs on right. Proceed to a locked red gate—10 feet to the left is an opening in the fence and a sign for the 6-mile Tolby Meadow trail. To explore more of the canyon, continue east 4 miles on U.S. 64 to Palisades Picnic Area, and 4 more miles to the end of canyon.*

Closest Town: Eagle Nest

Ownership: New Mexico Park and Recreation Division, (505) 377-6271; New Mexico Dept. of Game and Fish (505) 445-2311

20 | PHILMONT RANCH ROAD

Description: *AUTO TOUR.* The world-famous Philmont Scout Ranch encompasses 214 square miles of canyons, mountains, and grasslands—home to mule deer, elk, pronghorn, and native bison. No facilities along this route.

Viewing Information: From Cimarron, go 2 miles south on New Mexico Highway 21 to the hill which marks the bison enclosure on the right. As many as 135 bison may be seen along the next 0.9 mile. Occasional pronghorn inhabit the grasslands on either side of the road. Immediately south of the bison area, watch for deer in fields on both sides of the road for the next 0.5 mile; up to 150 deer may be seen feeding together. Best viewing times for bison are any time of day; deer are best seen at dawn/dusk. *VIEW FROM ROADSIDES ONLY; LANDS ON EITHER SIDE OF ROAD ARE PRIVATE PROPERTY.*

Directions: *From Cimarron, turn south onto New Mexico Highway 21 at Russell's One-Stop Shop and continue south 2 miles, where viewing begins.*

Closest Town: Cimarron

Ownership: Philmont Scout Ranch; Boy Scouts of America (505) 376-2281

21 | MAXWELL NATIONAL WILDLIFE REFUGE

Description: A visitor's first glimpse of Maxwell National Wildlife Refuge is a dark green line on the horizon where the Great Plains and Rocky Mountains meet. Deciduous groves of cottonwood, elm, and willow border many of the refuge's gravel roads. Three refuge lakes, called lakes 12, 13, and 14, respectively, are an important stopping place for waterfowl following a migration corridor along the Front Range of the Rocky Mountains.

Viewing Information: During peak migration in October, duck numbers can reach 52,000, with the greatest concentration of birds at Lake 12. Lake 13 affords good viewing for Canada geese and bald eagles November through March. American white pelicans are visiting the refuge in ever-increasing numbers, and may be seen June through October. Occasional viewing of sandhill cranes in October; occasional tundra swans. In May and June, look for a nesting colony of eared grebes at Lake 14. Good viewing of a black-tailed prairie dog town and occasional viewing of burrowing owls, just east of Lake 12 on the second access road. Occasional pronghorn in surrounding fields. Stop at visitor center for directions and refuge map. Bring insect repellent in summer.

Directions: Exit Interstate 25 at mile marker 426 and drive west 2 blocks into the village of Maxwell. Go 0.75 mile north on New Mexico Highway 445, then west on NM 505 for 2.5 miles to refuge entrance. Refuge headquarters is 1.25 miles north.

Closest Town: Maxwell

Ownership: U. S. Fish and Wildlife Service (505) 375-2331

The American Avocet breeds on mudflats, marshes, ponds, and alkaline lakes. Its head and neck is pinkish during breeding, turning pale gray in winter.
JOHN AND KAREN HOLLINGSWORTH

Description: Consisting of 100,000 acres between Costilla and Cimarron, Valle Vidal is a unit of the Carson National Forest, supervised by the Questa Ranger Station. It is the year-round home of about 1,700 elk, and one of the premier elk viewing sites in the state. The east side of the unit, east of the Taos/Colfax county line, is closed January 1 - March 31 for elk winter range protection. The area west of the county line is closed May 1 - June 31 for elk calving. The area opens July 1 each year to hiking and biking. *FUEL UP, CHECK TIRES, BRING WATER AND PROVISIONS.*

Viewing Information: Traveling west from Cimarron, best elk viewing beyond mile 44 along the gravel road, during pre-dawn or just after dusk. Watch for bison in the McCrystal Creek Campground area, at the 30.5 mile-mark; about 8.3 miles beyond lies Cimarron Campground; from this point heading west, elk viewing is excellent. About 1.25 miles west of the campground lies the pullout for Clayton Corrals and the actual *Valle Vidal*, a vast, grassy basin, rimmed by aspen- and fir-covered hills. Trail access for hikers and horseback is found at Clayton Corrals. The forest road beyond the *valle* also has good elk viewing. Occasional viewing of porcupine, Abert squirrel (most found on the east side of the Unit), mule deer, and black bear.

Directions: *See map at right. From Cimarron, take U.S. Highway 64 east. After traveling 4.7 miles, turn left (north) at the Valle Vidal Unit sign. This is a long, gravel road, well-maintained but rough in sections. From Taos, go north on NM 522 to Costilla. Turn right (east) on NM 196 which leads to viewing site.*

Closest Town: Cimarron (southeast entrance) and Amalia (northwest entrance)

Ownership: USDA Forest Service (505) 586-0520; New Mexico Dept. of Game and Fish (505) 445-2311

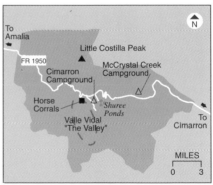

One hundred-thousand acres of forested hills and grassy meadows comprise the Valle Vidal Unit, year-round home to about 1,700 elk.

JERRY MONTGOMERY

REGION 3: GRASSLANDS and PRAIRIES

Dinosaurs once roamed this region of grass and sky, leaving behind tracks visible at Clayton Lake State Park. In the 1930s, the Dustbowl wreaked havoc in this region, causing a mass exodus of dryland farmers and ranchers. Today New Mexico's northeast prairies are returning to a healthy state. These vast grasslands now support populations of pronghorn, wild turkey, and mule deer. The area's playa, or intermittent, lakes provide important habitat for waterfowl and shorebirds.

Photo, opposite page: Kiowa National Grasslands. **MARK NOHL/NEW MEXICO DEPT. OF TOURISM**

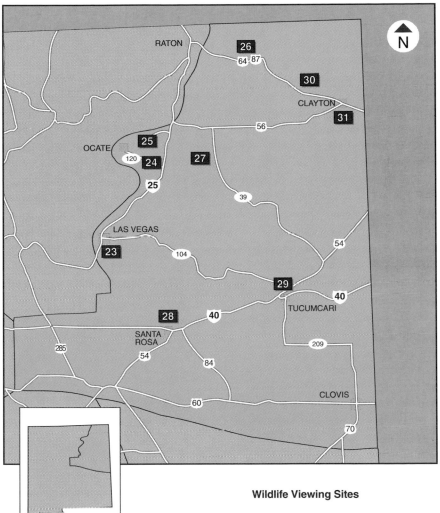

Wildlife Viewing Sites

23. Las Vegas National Wildlife Refuge, McAllister Lake
24. The Road to Wagon Mound
25. Charette Lakes
26. Capulin Volcano National Monument
27. Mills Canyon
28. Santa Rosa
29. Ladd S. Gordon Wildlife Area, Tucumcari Lake
30. Clayton Lake State Park
31. Kiowa Grassland, Unit 33

23 LAS VEGAS NATIONAL WILDLIFE REFUGE, McALLISTER LAKE

Description: These adjoining areas provide habitat for migrating waterfowl. Limited-access Las Vegas refuge is managed specifically for waterfowl. McAllister Lake is a popular fishing spot, with developed amenities, including restrooms, camping, a boat ramp, and parking.

Viewing Information: Both areas offer excellent viewing of bald eagle, Canada and snow geese, eared grebe, sandhill crane, and a diversity of waterfowl November through March, and shorebirds spring through fall. **At the refuge,** watch for Canada and snow geese, as well as sandhill cranes. On Sundays in November from 1 p.m. to 4:30 p.m., weather permitting, the refuge offers drive-by access to ponds and lands normally closed to the public. Hike the Gallinas Nature Trail, open 8 a.m. to 2 p.m. Monday through Friday, to view a nearby riparian woodland; a permit is required for entry and can be obtained at refuge office. The Crane Lake Overlook offers views of waterfowl and cranes at a distance. **McAllister Lake** is open year-round with free access, and hosts nesting yellow-headed blackbirds. *WATERFOWL HUNTING AT McALLISTER LAKE OCTOBER THROUGH JANUARY. LAKE CLOSED TO VEHICLES OCTOBER 31 THROUGH MARCH 1.*

Directions: *From Interstate 25 at the south edge of Las Vegas, New Mexico, turn east onto New Mexico Highway 104 and travel 1.2 miles. Turn right (south) onto NM 281. Drive 4 miles to refuge office, another 0.5 mile to Crane Lake overlook, and 3 more miles to McAllister Lake.*

Closest Town: Las Vegas (New Mexico)

Ownership: Las Vegas NWR, U.S. Fish & Wildlife Service (505) 425-3581; McAllister Lake, New Mexico Dept. of Game and Fish (505) 445-2311

AT McALLISTER LAKE   AT LAS VEGAS N. W. R.

Gregarious yellow-headed blackbirds nest in cattail and bulrush marshes. Their buzzing call resembles a rusty hinge.
DON L. MacCARTER

24 THE ROAD TO WAGON MOUND

Description: *AUTO TOUR.* This 19-mile stretch of road between Ocate and Wagon Mound affords some of the best pronghorn viewing in New Mexico. Grasslands lie on both sides of the road, with the Turkey Mountains to the southeast and Sangre de Cristo peaks to the west. The road culminates at Wagon Mound, where a small waterfowl area is located a half-mile north. No facilities along this route. *VIEW FROM ROADSIDES ONLY—LAND ALONG ROUTE IS PRIVATE PROPERTY.*

Viewing Information: Good to excellent year-round viewing of pronghorn between mile markers 22 and 38; best viewing from 4 p.m. to 9 p.m. in summer. Frequent summer viewing of coyote, golden eagle, ferruginous hawk, red-tailed hawk, Swainson's hawk, American kestrel, and meadowlark. Occasional migrating ducks at Wagon Mound Waterfowl Area October through November. Large swallow colony inhabits highway tunnel spring - summer.

Directions: *From Ocate to Wagon Mound along New Mexico Highway 120. At Wagon Mound, turn north on the frontage road and go 0.5 mile to Wagon Mound Wildlife Area sign and proceed through tunnel under freeway to site.*

Closest Town: Wagon Mound, Ocate

Ownership: Private property along New Mexico Highway 120; Wagon Mound Wildlife Area, New Mexico Dept. of Game and Fish (505) 445-2311

25 CHARETTE LAKES

Description: These 2 prairie lakes lie atop a remote mesa in prime pronghorn country. Some of the greatest concentrations of migratory waterfowl in the state occur here in late October. Bring water.

Viewing Information: More than 20,000 ducks may be seen September through November, with peak numbers in October; look for gadwall, American wigeon, northern pintail, teal species, and mallard, as well as diving ducks—redhead, canvasback, ringneck, and lesser scaup. Migrating bald eagles present October through November, and December through January. Watch for pronghorn, mule deer, and coyote on surrounding prairie. Lakes receive heavy use from anglers in June and early July.

Directions: *From Springer, travel 9.5 miles south on Interstate 25. Take exit 404 (Colmor) to New Mexico Highway 569, a graded road partially paved. At 8 miles, where New Mexico Dept. of Game and Fish sign marks the boundary, the road climbs sharply over a mesa to a rocky flat. Continue 5 miles to Charette Lakes.*

Closest Town: Springer

Ownership: New Mexico Dept. of Game and Fish (505) 445-2311

26 | CAPULIN VOLCANO NATIONAL MONUMENT

Description: Active just 10,000 years ago, Capulin Volcano rises 8,182 feet, cloaked in grassland and forest, including piñon and ponderosa pines, juniper, mountain mahogany, and chokecherry. It is said that the volcano was named *capulin* after the Spanish word for chokecherry. On a clear day, four states are visible from the highest point on the crater rim trail.

Viewing Information: Excellent viewing of mountain bluebird, black-headed grosbeak, chipping sparrow, Bewick's wren, horned lark, rufous-sided towhee, and mountain chickadee. Good early-morning viewing of mule deer year-round, wild turkey in summer and fall, and red-tailed hawk, turkey vulture, and porcupine in summer. Occasional viewing of gray fox, black bear, and thirteen-lined ground squirrel inside the crater area. Rattlesnakes seen frequently in summer. Golden eagle sightings possible year-round. The visitor center is open from 8:30 a.m. to 4:30 p.m.; the road to the rim is open from sunrise to sunset.

Directions: *Capulin lies within a triangle formed by the towns of Folsom, Des Moines, and Capulin, about 30 miles east of Raton. The entrance to the National Monument lies 3 miles north of the junction of U.S. Highway 64/87 and New Mexico Highway 325 at Capulin.*

Ownership: National Park Service (505) 278-2201

Four states are visible from the rim of this extinct volcano.
GARY RASMUSSEN

27 MILLS CANYON

Description: Mills Canyon is a beautiful surprise, opening up unexpectedly in the midst of rolling grasslands. Its varied terrain includes redrock canyon, piñon, juniper, and ponderosa pine, and a cottonwood riparian zone beside the Canadian River. Bring water.

Viewing Information: Occasional viewing of mule deer, wild turkey, red-tailed hawk, and other raptors year-round, as well as rock squirrel March through October. Good summer viewing of white-throated swift, hairy woodpecker, northern flicker, Say's phoebe, western wood pewee, Bewick's and canyon wren, and other songbirds. Look for the arid lands ribbon snake. Rare sightings of exotic Barbary sheep, which have lived along the Canadian River since the 1930s.

Directions: Travel 10 miles north of Roy on New Mexico Highway 39. Turn left (west) onto Forest Road 600 at the Mills Canyon Campground sign and continue 9 miles to the river. HIGH-CLEARANCE, FOUR-WHEEL-DRIVE VEHICLES RECOMMENDED; LAST 3 MILES OF ROAD IMPASSABLE IN WET WEATHER.

Closest Town: Roy

Ownership: USDA Forest Service (campground), (505) 374-9652; New Mexico State Land Office (adjacent lands), (505) 827-5033; Some private lands.

This black-tailed jackrabbit is a member of the hare family, of which there are four species in New Mexico. Their young are born fully furred with eyes open.
DON L. MacCARTER

28 SANTA ROSA

Description: This area includes Santa Rosa Lake, a seasonally-fluctuating reservoir of the Pecos River, and the Blue Hole, a limestone sinkhole. At Santa Rosa State Park, drive across the dam to the campground and walk 0.25 mile to the lake. A 0.75-mile barrier-free trail follows the river. In town, stop by 81-foot-deep Blue Hole, where an artesian spring gushes 3,000 gallons of water per minute.

Viewing Information: Occasional viewing of bald eagles and ring-billed gulls November through February—eagles roost on snags at water's edge, or on small islands in the lake. Barn swallows migrate through area in late March. Occasional sightings of coyote, mule deer, and pronghorn year-round; scaled quail and mourning dove fall and winter; migrating ospreys September - October; and waterfowl October through February. Best viewing time is fall.

Directions: *At Santa Rosa, go north under Interstate 40 overpass and follow access road New Mexico 91 north for 7 miles to the park. Blue Hole signs begin at 6th and Parker in Santa Rosa.*

Closest Town: Santa Rosa

Ownership: New Mexico Park & Recreaton Division (505) 472-3110; U. S. Army Corps of Engineers (505) 472-3115

29 LADD S. GORDON WILDLIFE AREA, TUCUMCARI LAKE

Description: Excellent shorebird habitat, Tucumcari Lake is a natural playa reservoir, the waters of which also serve local irrigation needs. The lake is rimmed by salt cedars, willows, and sedges along much of the shore.

Viewing Information: Very good viewing of diverse waterfowl, such as Canada and snow geese, and three species of teal, as well as mallard, canvasback, redhead, American wigeon, and northern pintail November through February. Shorebirds, best seen October through March, include the black-bellied plover, black-necked stilt, killdeer, American avocet, long-billed curlew, and several species of sandpiper. Spring and fall, watch for many songbirds, scaled quail, abundant Swainson's hawk, American kestrel, and other raptors.

Directions: *Take Mountain Road exit off Interstate 40 north into Tucumcari. At the intersection of Mountain Road and Main Street, turn east for 0.8 mile to the county road and sign for wildlife area. Continue north about 1 mile to the end of the road and turn west—road ends at wildlife area parking lot.*

Closest Town: Tucumcari

Ownership: New Mexico Dept. of Game and Fish (505) 445-2311

30 ▌CLAYTON LAKE STATE PARK

Description: Visitors to Clayton Lake can see evidence of wildlife that roamed this area roughly 100 million years ago. More than 500 preserved dinosaur tracks are here, left by at least 8 different kinds of dinosaurs on what was once the muddy bank of a vast inland sea.

Viewing Information: Watch for pronghorn along the road between town of Clayton and the lake; best viewing from dawn to 11 a.m. and 4 p.m. to dusk year-round. Once at the lake, take the left fork of the gravel road to Chicano Point to view Canada and snow geese, gadwall, northern pintail, lesser scaup, bufflehead, canvasback, redhead, and teal species November through March. Excellent early-morning viewing of mule deer year-round, with best viewing November through March. Occasional sightings of bald eagle October 15 through March 30.

Directions: *From Clayton, travel north 10.4 miles on New Mexico Highway 370 to the Clayton Lake turnoff; continue 1.5 miles to lake.*

Closest Town: Clayton

Ownership: New Mexico Park & Recreation Division (505) 374-8808

31 ▌KIOWA GRASSLAND, UNIT 33

Description: Unit 33 of the Kiowa Grasslands is a good example of an improving grassland and riparian site, recovering from the erosion of the Dust Bowl era. No facilities at this site.

Viewing Information: Occasional to good summer viewing of Swainson's hawk, American kestrel, long-billed curlew, northern bobwhite, scaled quail, mourning dove, western and eastern meadowlark, loggerhead shrike, lark bunting, and turkey vulture from mid-April through September. Occasional viewing of bald eagle November through March. Early mornings or late evenings, look for pronghorn, mule deer, raccoon, and gray fox year-round. Between May 1 and October 15, watch for rattlesnakes and Great Plains skink.

Directions: *From Clayton, drive 7 miles south on New Mexico Highway 402 (Nara Visa Highway). Turn left (east) onto an unmarked road and continue 5 miles, watching for a tiny brown sign marked, "Unit 33." Follow a sandy track onto the site, heading toward a windmill with parking at left. On foot, look north for a dark line of vegetation on the horizon which is Perico Creek. Walk about 0.5 mile towards the creek—STEP CAREFULLY OVER A LOW ELECTRIC FENCE.*

Closest Town: Clayton

Ownership: USDA Forest Service (505) 374-9652

REGION 4: SANDIAS and MANZANOS

These two mountain ranges mark the center of New Mexico. Sandia Crest rises 10,678 feet to the east of Albuquerque. To the south lie the Manzano Mountains, with broad plains flanking the range on either side. Both of these ranges are noted migration corridors for raptors, including the American kestrel, peregrine falcon, Cooper's and Swainson's hawk, golden eagle, and turkey vulture.

Photo, opposite page: Sandia Mountains. **JACK KELLY**

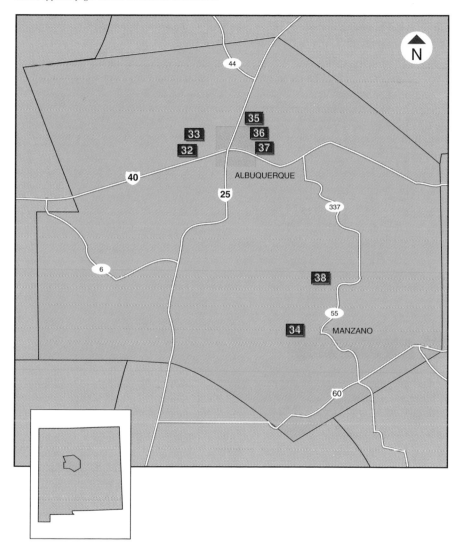

Wildlife Viewing Sites

32.   Rio Grande Nature Center
33.   Shady Lakes
34.   Manzano HawkWatch Site
35.   Elena Gallegos
36.   Sandia Crest
37.   Cienega Canyon
38.   Tajique Canyon

32 RIO GRANDE NATURE CENTER

Description: *URBAN SITE.* At the Rio Grande Nature Center, a network of nature trails winds through 100 acres of river-bottom woodlands. Known as the *bosque*, these willow, Russian olive, and century-old cottonwood trees provide viewing opportunities along the river. A cattail-rimmed pond attracts waterfowl and other birds. Outdoor viewing blinds and viewing room in the visitor center with a large glass wall overlook the pond. The center is devoted to quiet observation, with no picnicking, jogging, pets, or bikes allowed on site. A 1.5-mile bike trail is adjacent to the center.

Viewing Information: Excellent year-round viewing of Canada geese and mallard ducks, also migratory waterfowl November through February, including wood duck, ring-necked duck, gadwall, and American wigeon. Good viewing of painted turtle, greater roadrunner, red-winged blackbird, blue grosbeak, and cinnamon and green-winged teal in spring. Sandhill cranes visit November through January; pied-billed grebes present year-round. Nesting populations of killdeer, mourning dove, common nighthawk, black-chinned hummingbird, downy woodpecker, northern flicker, Say's phoebe, and Bewick's wren.

Directions: *In Albuquerque, from the intersection of Interstate 25 and Interstate 40 (known locally as the Big I Interchange), travel 2 miles west on I-40. Take Rio Grande Boulevard exit (157A) and continue 2 miles to Candelaria Street. Turn left and drive 1 mile to nature center entrance.*

Closest Town: Albuquerque

Ownership: New Mexico Park & Recreation Division, on land leased from Albuquerque Open Space (505) 344-7240

33 SHADY LAKES

Description: Acres of blooming water lilies, shaded by big cottonwoods and Russian olive trees, make Shady Lakes an idyllic spot for birding and other wildlife watching.

Viewing Information: Mid-May is a good time to visit, when water lilies are at their peak and wood ducks nest in cottonwoods at the far edge of the property. Also look for nesting great horned owls mid-February to mid-May. Summer birds include the American kestrel, Cooper's hawk, and belted kingfisher. Three turtle species (western painted, slider, and red-eared) may be seen, along with Woodhouse's toad, and gopher and garter snake. Fall colors and waterfowl in October. Call for special winter birding appointments.

Directions: *South of Bernalillo, take Tramway Boulevard exit (234) off Interstate 25 and drive west 1.5 miles to New Mexico Highway 313. Turn right and continue 0.5 mile to Shady Lakes sign.*

Closest Town: Bernalillo

Ownership: Shady Lakes Water Lily Gardens, (505) 898-2568 or 898-8531

34 | MANZANO HAWKWATCH SITE

Description: High on Capilla Peak in the Manzano Mountains, migrating raptors fly close to the crest each fall. This site also offers striking scenery with top-of-the-world views. Binoculars or a spotting scope is essential. No facilities—bring water, sunscreen, and food.

Viewing Information: *SEASONAL VIEWING.* Migrating raptors pass through between September 10 and October 20. A wide variety of migrating and resident hawks, eagles, and falcons may be seen above and below the crest; it is not unusual to see 150 raptors on a good day, weather permitting. Trained observers on-site daily September - October. For more information, contact HawkWatch International, Inc., P.O. Box 35706, Albuquerque, NM 87176-5706.

Directions: *From Manzano, take the first right onto dirt Forest Road 245 directly across from the church. Stay to the right, following signs for New Canyon and Capilla Peak camprounds. The road ends in 9 miles at the entrance to second campground, below the fire tower. Park off the road, 200 yards before fire tower road, and hike west across the meadow. Hike 20-30 minutes on the Gavilan Trail, which follows the ridge northwest to the observation site.*

Closest Town: Manzano

Ownership: USDA Forest Service (505) 847-2990; Project directed by HawkWatch International, (505) 255-7622, FAX 255-1775

35 | ELENA GALLEGOS

Description: This 640-acre site is outstanding grasslands-woodlands habitat at the edge of suburban Albuquerque. A hiking/horseback trail leads to a viewing blind near a small, spring-fed pond. The park's Domingo Baca Trail leads to an area of favored browse for mule deer. Mountain bike trails crisscross the area.

Viewing Information: Early mornings in fall are best times for viewing; avoid high-use periods in summer, weekends, and holidays. Summer temperatures typically reach the high 90s. Very good viewing of piñon jay, red-tailed hawk, mountain bluebird, towhee species, Bewick's wren, mule deer, rock squirrel, scaled quail, and black-tailed jackrabbit. Occasional viewing of burrowing and great horned owl, greater roadrunner, pied-billed grebe, and wood duck and other waterfowl in season, along with porcupine, coyote, and raccoon. Rare sightings of mountain lion at the pond area.

Directions: *Approaching Albuquerque from the north, take the Tramway Road exit (234) off Interstate 25. The road gradually climbs 7.5 miles, eventually paralleling the mountains. Pass 1 stop sign and 2 stoplights; about 0.5 mile beyond San Rafael Street, turn left at the sign to the park. From downtown Albuquerque, travel north on Tramway Boulevard from Montgomery; 0.8 mile to entrance on right.*

Closest Town: Albuquerque

Ownership: City of Albuquerque, Open Space Division (505) 873-6620

36 | SANDIA CREST

Description: Watch the life zones change on this drive, from an area of ponderosa pines and spring-flowering locust trees to mixed conifers, culminating in spruce-fir forests atop 10,678-foot Sandia Crest. A barrier-free trail leads to a rim overlook with incredible views. A second trail follows the rim and dips into conifer forest, while still another trail explores the steep face of the crest. Visit May through October—site is otherwise inaccessible due to heavy snow.

Viewing Information: Best viewing is mid-week, early morning or late evening; be prepared for high visitor usage most other times. Good viewing of many warbler species, and many other birds, including hermit thrush, rosy and Cassin's finch, red crossbill, pine grosbeak, Clark's nutcracker, white-throated swift, pine siskin, and common raven. Mammals include Abert and red squirrel, least and Colorado chipmunk, and mule deer. Occasional viewing of eagles and other raptors soaring near summit. Uncommon sightings of black bear, of which this area has a large and viable population.

Directions: *See directions to Cienega Canyon (site 37), just downslope along the same road. From the New Mexico Highway 536 junction at the Cienega Canyon turnoff, continue 12 miles up the paved main road to the crest.*

Closest Town: Cedar Crest

Ownership: USDA Forest Service (505) 281-3304

37 | CIENEGA CANYON

Description: Nestled amid mixed conifers and ponderosa pines, this riparian area provides an excellent outdoor setting for the physically challenged, as well as for other visitors. A stream passes through woods and meadow, while the forested slopes of Sandia Peak's eastern face rise on three sides. Part of a national recreation trail, with excellent barrier-free facilities and interpretive signs in print and Braille.

Viewing Information: Occasional viewing of Abert squirrels, the site's official "mascots." Good viewing of mule deer, northern flicker, scrub and Steller's jay, rufous-sided towhee, black-headed grosbeak, junco, western tanager, broad-tailed hummingbird, and other species. Warbler species include Audubon's, yellow-rumped, Virginia's, and Grace's. Outstanding fall colors.

Directions: *From Interstate 40, take the Tijeras/New Mexico Highway 337 exit 6 miles east of Albuquerque—watch for NM 14 sign as you exit. Travel north on NM14 for 6 miles to the junction of NM 536 (Sandia Crest Road). Continue 1.6 miles on Sandia Crest Rd., then turn left at the Sulphur Canyon/Cienega Canyon sign. Drive 0.5 mile, turning right at Cienega Canyon sign; parking area is 0.5 mile ahead on right.*

Closest Town: Albuquerque

Ownership: USDA Forest Service (505) 281-3304

Description: This area is unusual for its thick concentrations of deciduous woodlands, particularly Rocky Mountain and bigtooth maples, which blaze red with fall colors. Aspen, willow, ponderosa pine, and other montane flora is also found in this canyon on the east flank of the Manzano Mountains.

Viewing Information: Migrating raptors are a major attraction here September through November. Between the towns of Estancia and Tajique, scan fenceposts and telephone poles for hawks, including Swainson's, ferruginous, red-tailed, and other species; golden eagle, American kestrel, and prairie falcon may also be seen along the way. In the canyon woodlands, watch for fall migrating warblers and other birds, such as the band-tailed pigeon, white-throated swift, western tanager, black-headed and evening grosbeak, and green-tailed towhee. Look for Merriam's turkey July through October; New Mexico milk snake may also be seen. Best viewing is mid-week, because of high visitor usage at 4th of July Campground area.

Directions: *From the southern edge of Estancia, travel west on New Mexico Highway 55 about 13.5 miles to the village of Tajique. Turn right onto Forest Road 55 at the 4th of July Campground sign—this begins a 20-mile gravel road loop. After 7 miles, take right fork to 4th of July Campground. Return to main road to complete loop; gravel road becomes more primitive after campground. The Bosque Trailhead lies 3 miles beyond road fork. To finish loop and return to the highway, keep left at another road fork 4 miles beyond the trailhead.*

Closest Town: Estancia

Ownership: USDA Forest Service (505) 847-2990

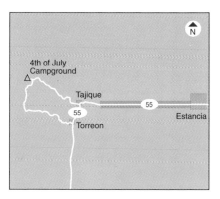

The secretive New Mexico milk snake can be found under logs, stumps, rocks and boards.
CHARLES PAINTER

REGION 5: GILA COUNTRY

Some of the most rugged mountains in New Mexico are found in this region, an area known for its diversity of bird species. Many mammals also live here, including Rocky Mountain bighorn sheep, Rocky Mountain elk, mule deer, ringtail, and javelina. Nearly one-fourth of the 3,300,000-acre Gila National Forest is designated wilderness. The largest of these is the Gila Wilderness, promoted by conservationist Aldo Leopold and set aside in 1924—the first official wilderness area in the United States.

Photo, opposite page: Turkey Creek. DON L. MacCARTER

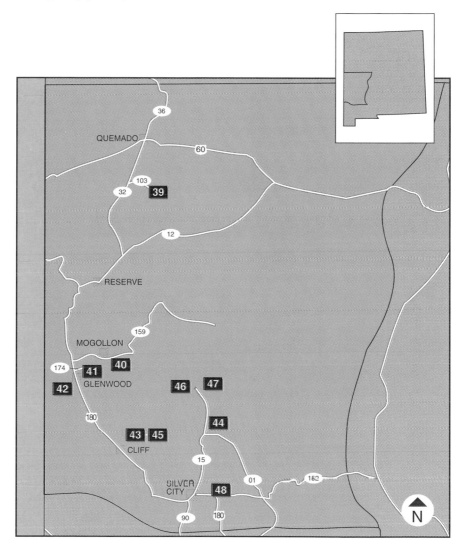

Wildllife Viewing Sites

39.	Quemado Lake	44.	Lake Roberts
40.	Mogollon, Willow Creek, Snow Lake	45.	Turkey Creek Road
41.	The Catwalk, Glenwood Fish Hatchery	46.	The Road to the Cliff Dwellings
42.	San Francisco Box, Dugway Canyon	47.	Heart Bar Riparian Area
43.	Gila Riparian Preserve	48.	Fort Bayard

39 QUEMADO LAKE

Description: The forested hills of the Apache National Forest surround Quemado Lake, a small reservoir popular for trout fishing and recreation. At the dam, follow Fishing Trail to the lake's marshy east end to look for waterfowl, songbirds, and migrating bald eagles.

Viewing Information: Occasional viewing of nesting red-winged and yellow-headed blackbird spring and summer; waterfowl November through February; and migrating bald eagles in winter and early spring. Soras may be seen spring and summer. Good viewing of belted kingfisher, mountain bluebird, and many other songbirds in summer. Other breeding birds include green-winged teal, pied-billed grebe, northern rough-winged and violet-green swallow, and mallard. Look for mountain tree frog and golden-mantled ground squirrel. Elk may also be seen, usually late evenings above the lake.

Directions: *Drive 0.5 mile west of Quemado on U.S. Highway 60, then turn left (south) onto New Mexico Highway 32 and proceed 14 miles. Turn left (east) on NM 103 and continue 4 miles to lake.*

Closest Town: Quemado

Ownership: USDA Forest Service (505) 773-4678

40 MOGOLLON, WILLOW CREEK, SNOW LAKE

Description: This narrow, winding road into the Mogollon Mountains climbs to an area of high mountain meadows. The route ends at Snow Lake and 8,598-foot Negrito Mountain. A high-clearance vehicle is recommended for this drive, which takes at least half a day to complete. *FUEL UP AND BRING PROVISIONS. NO SERVICES ALONG ROUTE.*

Viewing Information: Good birding at the three Willow Creek campgrounds—watch for the three-toed woodpecker, hermit thrush, Townsend's solitaire, ruby-crowned kinglet, blue grouse, red-faced warbler, and band-tailed pigeon. Excellent dawn/dusk roadside viewing of elk at higher elevations, especially near Negrito Mountain north of Snow Lake. Occasional viewing of mule deer, wild turkey, as well as red and Abert squirrel. Area can be exceptional for wildflowers.

Directions: *Four miles north of Glenwood, turn right (east) on New Mexico Highway 159—road is usually open June through October, paved to the village of Mogollon and gravel thereafter. Follow NM 159 to Willow Creek Campgrounds. To reach Snow Lake, take the middle fork of three gravel roads at the junction 2.5 miles beyond the campgrounds; then turn right onto Forest Road 142. DRIVE IS STEEP, NARROW, WINDING; DO NOT ATTEMPT WITH TRAILER OR RV.*

Closest Town: Glenwood

Ownership: USDA Forest Service (505) 533-6231

Description: This catwalk, a causeway built along a canyon wall, passes through a scenic riparian area of white-trunked sycamore trees and cottonwoods beside Whitewater Creek, in the shadow of rugged cliffs and massive boulders. Adjacent to this site, the wooded grounds of the Glenwood Fish Hatchery afford good birding.

Viewing Information: Visit the catwalk midweek, at dawn or dusk, for best wildlife viewing—weekends are crowded. Scan the cliffs for Rocky Mountain bighorn sheep; early mornings they are often seen on the trail and in the picnic area. *DO NOT APPROACH SHEEP.* Commonly-seen birds include American dipper, golden eagle, violet-green swallow, white-throated swift, several warbler species, orioles, canyon and rock wren, painted redstart, and western tanager. Occasional viewing of raccoons, snakes, and tree frogs. Mountain lion and black bear present, though rarely seen. At the hatchery, look for the common black hawk—rare in this area—and tiny Arizona coral snake. Hatchery is also a good spot for winter waterfowl.

Directions: *From Glenwood, turn east onto New Mexico Highway 174 and go 0.2 mile, watching for gravel road to fish hatchery on right—sign is hard to see and often missed. To visit catwalk, return to NM 174 and continue east 5 miles—road ends at Whitewater Picnic Ground and the start of catwalk. Visitors must cross Whitewater Creek twice by vehicle; be aware of high water at times. Follow a marked trail leading from the picnic area to the causeway and beyond.*

Closest Town: Glenwood

Ownership: USDA Forest Service (505) 539-2481; New Mexico Dept. of Game and Fish, Glenwood Fish Hatchery (505) 539-2461 or 524-6090

It usually takes eight to ten weeks for a young golden eagle to fledge.
CARY HULL

42 SAN FRANCISCO BOX, DUGWAY CANYON

Description: The San Francisco River and nearby South Dugway Canyon are fine examples of Southwestern desert and riparian habitats still relatively intact. At the river, walk a half-mile downstream to enter the "box." This area has escaped heavy livestock grazing and retains much of its native flora, including both the Fremont and narrow-leaf cottonwood, as well as a hybrid of the two, and Arizona sycamore, mesquite, and walnut trees. One mile south along U.S. Highway 180, a turnout near the bridge over South Dugway Canyon is an excellent spot for viewing Rocky Mountain bighorn sheep.

Viewing Information: At the river: View an active swallow colony across the river from parking area. Good viewing of mule deer, rock squirrel, jackrabbit, beaver, and great blue heron. Common black hawks nest here; Rocky Mountain bighorn sheep may also be seen. Mid-April through mid-June, and again in fall, many birds inhabit hybrid cottonwood stands, including Cordilleran flycatcher, western kingbird, violet-green swallow, black phoebe, northern oriole, and western and summer tanager, among others. Watch for the Gila spotted whiptail lizard. *BRING WATER. MID-SUMMER TEMPERATURES OVER 100 DEGREES.* At **South Dugway Bridge**, scan the western hillsides for Rocky Mountain bighorn sheep, javelina, golden eagle, and mule deer.

Directions: *To reach river and "box," travel 5 miles south of Glenwood on U.S. 180. Turn right onto Forest Road 519 at San Francisco Hot Springs sign, and follow dirt track about 1 mile to turnaround, also used as a campground. (Note: some of this area is private land.) The Dugway bridge turnoff is about a mile south of the junction of FR 519 and U.S. 180, just north of mile marker 57.*

Closest Town: Glenwood

Ownership: USDA Forest Service (505) 539-2481

San Francisco Box affords good birding, especially in its riverside, hybrid cottonwood groves. DON L. MacCARTER

43 GILA RIPARIAN PRESERVE

Description: Managed jointly by The Nature Conservancy and Forest Service, this site is a patchwork of 300 acres where Mogollon Creek meets the Gila, New Mexico's last major free-flowing river. No facilities at this site.

Viewing Information: Visit mid-week, early morning or late evening, for best birding; site is often crowded on weekends. Watch for Cordilleran flycatcher, yellow-breasted chat, western wood pewee, northern cardinal, pyrrhuloxia, three species of tanager, vermillion flycatcher, and Bell's and solitary vireo. Sandhill cranes may be seen in winter.

Directions: From Cliff, take New Mexico Highway 211 north 1 mile. Take the left fork at NM 293 (Box Canyon Road). Continue 5 miles on paved road and 2 miles on gravel road to the river. Park at first pullout—sandy riverside tracks become treacherous farther on. Walk upstream along Mogollon Creek to access one portion of the preserve; a second section lies along the Gila River, just downstream from the Mogollon Creek influx.

Closest Town: Cliff

Ownership: Jointly managed by The Nature Conservancy (505) 988-3867 and USDA Forest Service (505) 538-2771

44 LAKE ROBERTS

Description: Surrounded by pine-covered hills, this small, constructed lake lies amid a variety of micro-habitats: marshy east shore, rocky canyon wash, piñon-juniper mesa, and nearby pine flats.

Viewing Information: The shallow east end of Lake Roberts supports a cattail-willow thicket and small islet, with good viewing of red-winged blackbird, marsh wren, killdeer, song sparrow, Virginia rail, sora, pied-billed grebe, wintering waterfowl, and osprey and bald eagle during migration. Good area for hummingbirds May through September, including the broad-tailed, rufous, and black-chinned. Mule deer, elk, and wild turkey inhabit "piney flats" just east of the lake on New Mexico Highway 35, with excellent year-round viewing pre-dawn and just after dusk.

Directions: Travel north of Silver City on NM 15 about 25 miles to the junction with NM 35. Turn right (east) onto NM 35 and proceed 4 miles to settlement of Lake Roberts. An alternate route, recommended for RVs and motor homes, is to take NM 152 east of Silver City 18 miles to junction with NM 35. Turn left onto NM 35 and travel 29 miles to Lake Roberts.

Closest Town: Silver City

Ownership: New Mexico Dept. of Game and Fish (505) 524-6090

45 TURKEY CREEK ROAD

Description: *AUTO TOUR.* This winding, 15-mile gravel road climbs to a panoramic view of the Gila Wilderness, then drops down to a riparian oasis beside the Gila River. Massive cottonwoods and sycamores grow beside the river beneath ochre-colored crags and rugged mountains. No facilities along this route, which passes through some of the more scenic country in southwestern New Mexico. Plan on a half-day to complete this drive, a round-trip of 30 miles. A four-wheel-drive vehicle is recommended. *DO NOT ATTEMPT DRIVE IN WINTER.*

Viewing Information: Bring binoculars or a spotting scope, and visit midweek, early morning or late evening, for best viewing. Scan the crags for abundant Rocky Mountain bighorn sheep, and occasional javelina, Arizona gray squirrel, and mule deer. Good viewing for raptors, including golden eagle, zone-tailed hawk, and common black hawk in summer, and bald eagle in winter. Also look for solitary vireo, several species of flycatcher, western and summer tanager, northern cardinal, and other songbirds. Mountain lion and black bear present, though rarely seen.

Directions: *From Gila, follow New Mexico Highway 211 for 1 mile, and turn left (north) at Turkey Creek Road (NM 153). Drive to summit, then descend to the river—there are numerous pullouts for parking. FORD RIVER IN LATE SUMMER ONLY, WITH FOUR-WHEEL-DRIVE VEHICLE ONLY. DO NOT ATTEMPT OTHERWISE. Road continues 1 mile, ending at wilderness entrance.*

Closest Town: Gila

Ownership: USDA Forest Service (505) 538-2771

Rocky Mountain bighorn sheep can get along with a minimum of free-standing water, obtaining moisture instead from snow, dew, and vegetation. DON L. MacCARTER

Description: *AUTO TOUR.* Scenic New Mexico Highway 15 winds through forests, mesas, and mountains, ending at the site of ancient Mogollon Indian cliff dwellings. The Clinton Anderson Overlook, near the end of the route, affords spectacular views of the forested mountains of the Gila Wilderness.

Viewing Information: Gila Cliff Dwellings National Monument opens to the public at 8 a.m. in summer, 9 a.m. in winter—begin this tour by 6:30 a.m. or earlier for best wildlife viewing along the way. Very good viewing of mule deer and wild turkey near the Clinton Anderson Overlook and the Heart Bar Wildlife Area. Look for great blue herons and occasional beaver activity at the Scorpion Campgrounds near the river, just past the visitor center on right. Along the river, enjoy good viewing of red-tailed hawk, turkey vulture, American kestrel, and other raptors spring through fall. Occasional bald eagles in winter. Very good viewing of four jay species, red-faced warbler, canyon wren, Bell's vireo, mule deer, and several squirrel species, including the Abert squirrel. Mountain king snake in area. Rare sightings of javelina, mountain lion, and black bear. Most comfortable viewing temperatures are in spring and fall; summer temperatures typically climb to the high 90s.

Directions: *About 41 miles north of Silver City on New Mexico Highway 15 to the Gila Cliff Dwellings. Narrow, winding, road, paved the entire way.*

Closest Town: Silver City

Ownership: USDA Forest Service (505) 536-2250; National Park Service (505) 536-9344

The song of the canyon wren is frequently heard amid the rocky hillsides at the cliff dwelling area.
DON L. MacCARTER

47 HEART BAR RIPARIAN AREA

Description: The Heart Bar Ranch, acquired by the New Mexico Department of Game and Fish more than four decades ago, includes access to two riparian areas along the West Fork of the Gila River. One area is Little Creek Pond, with rushes, willow thickets, and cattails, flanked by tall cottonwoods on the west and rocky hills overlooking the river to the east. Another 1.5 miles down the road, an unmarked dirt track leads to a riverside cottonwood grove.

Viewing Information: Spring through fall at Little Creek Pond, look for black-headed grosbeak, yellow-breasted chat, solitary vireo, painted redstart, mallard, common merganser, rail species, sora, various warblers, also beaver and muskrat. A great blue heron rookery is visible directly across from the Heart Bar ranch house, in pine trees along the south side of highway. Occasional migrating bald eagles in winter, and ospreys spring and fall. Sporadic year-round viewing of bobcat, gray fox, wild turkey, and coyote at dawn/dusk; rare sightings of mountain lion. The common black hawk has been sighted here. Watch for Rocky Mountain bighorn sheep on hillsides above river. The narrowhead garter snake is common.

Directions: *Take New Mexico Highway 15 north of Silver City about 30 miles. Look for the tiny settlement of Gila Hot Springs, and start counting mileage from the Gila Hot Springs Store. Continue 1.3 miles north of the store to sign for Little Creek. Just past sign, pull off road on right and look for a trail encircling the pond. Another 1.5 miles north along NM 15 look for a dirt track to the right, just beyond mile marker 41; the track is flanked by wooden poles on each side.*

Closest Town: Gila Hot Springs

Ownership: New Mexico Dept. of Game and Fish
(505) 524-6090

Among the most common of rails, the secretive sora frequents marshes with dense vegetation. Its call is a musical descending 'whinny.' JOHN AND KAREN HOLLINGSWORTH

Description: This site is a good example of Upper Sonoran life zone habitat. Piñon/juniper and grasslands at the south end of the area give way to ponderosa pine and Gambel oak woodlands where the property meets the mountains.

Viewing Information: Excellent roadside viewing of elk, in pre-dawn or just after sunset—elk may be seen year-round, but are best viewed winter and spring. Visit in May when yucca plants bloom and elk devour the flowering stalks. Some of the best viewing on foot is found along the Cameron Creek Trail. Very good year-round viewing of Coue's white-tailed deer, especially around the hospital grounds. Good to excellent viewing of tarantula, many lizard species, coyote, jackrabbit, and mule deer year-round. Good viewing of red-tailed and Cooper's hawk, Montezuma quail, band-tailed pigeon, great horned and long-eared owl, wild turkey, western and Cassin's kingbird, chipping sparrow, and the plain titmouse, April through September. Occasional viewing of bobcat, badger, black bear, and porcupine.

Directions: *Travel 6.5 miles east of Silver City on U.S. Highway 180. Turn left at the Fort Bayard/Central intersection and continue 0.5 mile to the main gate. Enter the grounds, watching for a series of small brown Forest Road 536 signs, posted at frequent intervals among buildings. Follow signs past buildings and continue 3 miles on gravel road. Cross a cattleguard, pass the Forest Service site on right, and turn left at the National Recreation Trails Road. Go 0.25 mile to a small parking lot—5 hiking trails start here, including Cameron Creek.*

Closest Town: Silver City

Ownership: USDA Forest Service (505) 538-2771; U. S. Army (national cemetery); State of New Mexico (hospital and fort); New Mexico Dept. of Game and Fish (wildlife refuge)

The red-tailed hawk, a large, broad-winged buteo, occurs in both light and dark phases in New Mexico.
DON L. MacCARTER

REGION 6: SOUTHERN RIO GRANDE VALLEY

One of the great rivers of the Southwest, the legendary Rio Grande, appears today in a much-altered version. Most of its cottonwood *bosques,* or riverside woodlands, are gone. The Rio Grande continues to function as an important wintering area: bald eagles, thousands of snow geese, ducks, sandhill cranes, and a few extremely rare whooping cranes stop here during migration. Areas of wild beauty may still be found here, including the rugged Organ Mountains east of the Rio Grande, and scattered remnants of *bosque* and wetlands.

Photo, opposite page: The Rio Grande. **DON L. MacCARTER**

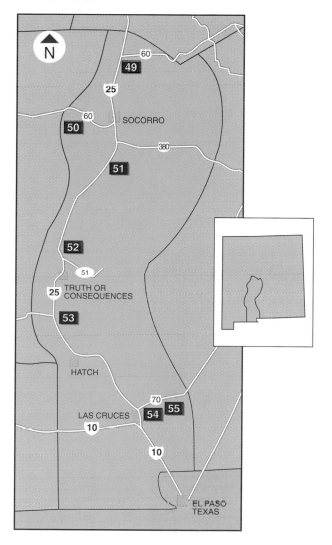

49 LA JOYA REFUGE

Description: This 3,550-acre wetlands area consists of six interconnected ponds, divided by levee access roads.

Viewing Information: Excellent viewing of migratory waterfowl March through August, especially teal species, mallard, lesser scaup, northern shoveler, gadwall, and goose species. Many summer songbirds. Good viewing of Gambel's quail, ring-necked pheasant, raccoon, and coyote year-round; raptors spring and fall. Pied-billed grebe, double-crested cormorant, sora, Virginia rail, green-backed heron, black-necked stilt, American avocet, and other shorebirds are present November-February. *WILDLIFE VIEWING DISCOURAGED SEPTEMBER THROUGH MID-JANUARY DUE TO HUNTING.*

Directions: *From Interstate 25, take exit 169. Continue on gravel road to cattleguard. Continue 0.5 mile and take left fork to uninhabited stone house—use care at a sandy arroyo crossing along the way. House sits on an overlook—park here and walk 0.25 mile downhill to the water. DO NOT ATTEMPT OTHER AREA ROADS DUE TO DEEP SAND. VACANT HOUSE IS PRIVATE PROPERTY—PLEASE DON'T TRESPASS.*

Closest Town: Socorro

Ownership: New Mexico Dept. of Game and Fish (505) 841-8881

When alarmed, this immature green-backed heron elevates its shaggy crest.
DON L. MacCARTER

Description: South Baldy Peak rises 10,783 feet from a grassy plain. Along its north face lies Water Canyon, bordered on the east by rugged, red-rock cliffs.

Viewing Information: Excellent year-round viewing of pronghorn, ferruginous hawk, and golden eagle between New Mexico Highway 60 and Water Canyon Campground. Good to excellent viewing of acorn woodpecker, white-throated swift, black-chinned hummingbird, western wood pewee, ash-throated flycatcher, mountain chickadee, solitary and warbling vireo, lazuli bunting, black-throated gray warbler, and other birds in spring and summer. Best birding at campground, and from canyon to crest. Occasional viewing of wild turkey and mule deer in campground in winter, and near summit in summer.

Directions: *Take NM 60 west from Socorro 12.5 miles. Turn left (south) at Water Canyon Campground sign onto Forest Road 235. Drive 4.5 miles to campground. Pavement ends here, but unpaved FR 235 continues to Langmuir Laboratory gate at South Baldy mountain for panoramic views. A high-clearance vehicle is recommended for unpaved portion of road.*

Closest Town: Socorro

Ownership: USDA Forest Service (505) 854-2281

The acorn woodpecker is easily identified by its Harlequin face and whitish eyes. It habitually stores acorns in the bark of trees.
LARRY BROCK

51 | BOSQUE DEL APACHE NATIONAL WILDLIFE REFUGE

Description: This important refuge is home to 320 species of birds and a great diversity of mammals, reptiles, and amphibians. Chihuahuan Desert uplands, marshes, small lakes, constructed waterways, and agricultural land are bordered by ancient cottonwoods, most often in *bosques,* or riverside woods. At the southern end of this refuge, the Chupadera Mountains rise to the west, while San Pascual Mountain and the Sierra Oscuras can be seen to the east. Observation platforms and hiking trails on site. A private campground is located on the refuge's northern boundary.

Viewing Information: Strong possibility of seeing the rare and federally-listed endangered whooping crane. As many as 6 of these stately birds typically arrive with sandhill cranes in late November, and stay through January. Early December through January is peak time for viewing most other wildlife here. Just before sunrise to about 9 a.m. is best time to view wintering cranes and geese. Excellent viewing for up to 17,000 greater and lesser sandhill cranes, and as many as 57,000 snow geese, including Ross', in late fall through early winter. Occasional sightings of tundra swans. Excellent viewing of Gambel's quail, pyrrhuloxia, and white-crowned sparrow from the indoor viewing area of the visitor center. Good viewing for Canada geese and a variety of ducks October through April. Mule deer, coyote, raptors, and wild turkey may be seen year-round; songbirds, shore, and wading birds are present spring and summer. The Festival of Cranes, a four-day annual event held the third weekend of November, provides once-a-year guided tours of areas not usually open to the public. Call for details.

Directions: *From Socorro, take Interstate 25 south to exit 139 (San Antonio). Drive 8 miles south on New Mexico Highway 1 from village of San Antonio. Approaching refuge from the south, take freeway exit 124 (San Marcial) and go 9 miles north on NM 1 to entrance.*

Closest Town: Socorro

Ownership: U. S. Fish & Wildlife Service
(505) 835-1828

The federally-endangered whooping cranes at Bosque Del Apache NWR were raised by foster-parent sandhill cranes at Grays Lake NWR in Idaho.
DON L. MacCARTER

52 | NORTH MONTICELLO POINT

Description: Set against the rugged Fra Cristobal Range, Elephant Butte Lake is a popular recreation spot in summer. However, some areas of the lake, including North Monticello Point, are more secluded and undeveloped.

Viewing Information: American white pelicans may be seen sporadically in winter. Bald eagles are present November through March, with highest numbers in January. Occasional viewing of water/marsh bird species along mudflats during spring and fall migration. Viewing of double-crested and olivaceous cormorant, and western and Clark's grebe in summer; ring-billed gull and duck species during winter; and tern species during migration. Visit mid week; avoid weekends and holidays. Summer temperatures typically reach high 90s.

Directions: *North of Truth or Consequences on Interstate 25, take Exit 92 (Mitchell Point). On the gravel road, watch for signs to North Monticello Point. Take the gravel road about 6 miles to the fork, turning left (north) where road dead-ends in the water. Right fork goes to North Monticello Point developed area.*

Closest Town: Truth or Consequences

Ownership: New Mexico Park & Recreation Division (505) 744-5421

53 | CABALLO LAKE STATE PARK, PERCHA DAM STATE PARK

Description: Caballo Lake is a long, narrow reservoir of the Rio Grande, bounded by the rugged Caballo Mountains to the east and surrounded by Chihuahuan Desert. Just south of Caballo lies Percha Dam State Park with good birding.

Viewing Information: Visit sites mid-week for best viewing; holidays and weekends can be crowded. Caballo Lake offers excellent viewing of bald eagles by car, foot, or boat, October through February; about 40 eagles winter here, with another 60 in nearby waters. Watch for eagles perched on snags or soaring over the water. Also look for gull, cormorant, grebe, and waterfowl species, as well as American white pelican and sandhill crane. A fully-developed, high-traffic site, Percha Dam still offers good birding for unusual species.

Directions: *About 16 miles south of Truth or Consequences on Interstate 25, take exit 59. Follow signs to either Caballo Lake State Park on left, or Percha Dam State Park on right.*

Closest Town: Truth or Consequences

Ownership: New Mexico Park & Recreation Division (505) 743-3942

54 DRIPPING SPRINGS NATURAL AREA

Description: At the edge of rolling Chihuahuan Desert grasslands, this picturesque area of rocky peaks, narrow canyons, and open woodlands shelters the
Dripping Springs Natural Area, noted for its "weeping walls" during summer
rainstorms. Formerly known as the Cox Ranch, this area encompasses a
wealth of habitats containing great biological diversity, including 4 endemic
wildflower species, the endangered Organ Mountains evening primrose and
other rare plants, and a race of the Colorado chipmunk.

Viewing Information: Excellent year-round viewing of red-tailed hawk,
Gambel's quail, and rock squirrel. Very good viewing of desert mule deer and
coyote year-round. Good viewing of golden eagle spring and summer. Also
watch for black-throated sparrow, ladder-backed woodpecker, verdin, black-
tailed gnatcatcher, lesser nighthawk, Scott's oriole, cactus wren, desert cotton-
tail, and collared and tree lizard in spring and summer. Occasional sightings of
mountain lion, of which this area has a viable population.

Directions: *From Interstate 25 in Las Cruces, take the University Exit. Travel east
9 miles on University Avenue (County Road 77) to site. Watch for signs to A. B.
Cox Visitor Center at the preserve. No admittance after 3 p.m.; gate closes at 8
p.m. It's a 1.5 mile hike to the springs.*

Closest Town: Las Cruces

Ownership: Bureau of Land Management (505) 525-4300 in cooperation with
The Nature Conservancy (505) 522-1219

*The rock-dwelling collared lizard frequents canyons and areas where vegetation
is sparse. It uses boulders for basking and lookouts.* DON L. MacCARTER

AGUIRRE SPRING

Description: At Aguirre Spring Campground, the high mountain wall of the Organ Needles curves dramatically around a semicircle of Chihuahuan Desert habitat. The campground is nestled at the base of spectacular cliffs, overlooking the Tularosa Basin and White Sands National Monument. Alligator juniper, gray oak, mountain mahogany, and sotol are a few of the abundant plant species here. Seasonal springs and streams occur in the canyon bottoms, with a few perennial springs that support riparian habitats.

Viewing Information: Spring through fall, best wildlife viewing is in early morning, late afternoon, or at night. Good birding; watch for red-tailed hawk, acorn woodpecker, canyon towhee, canyon and rock wren, Scott's oriole, and black-chinned hummingbird. Good viewing of lizard species, including tree, collared, and Chihuahuan whiptail. Also look for Great Plains skink, mountain patch-nosed snake, western diamondback rattlesnake, rock squirrel, Texas antelope squirrel, and Colorado chipmunk. Abundant tiger swallowtail butterflies on purple thistle blooms in summer. Occasional viewing of mule deer, gray fox, and ringtail. Rare sightings of mountain lion, banded rock rattlesnake, and prairie falcon. In winter, wildlife is more active during the warmest part of the day. Winter birds include dark-eyed junco, rufous-sided towhee, bluebird and jay species, loggerhead shrike, and numerous raptors, including golden eagle and American kestrel.

Directions: *From Interstate 25 in Las Cruces, take U.S. Highway 70/82 about 13 miles east to San Augustin Pass. Turn right 2 miles from the pass at the BLM sign for the Aguirre Spring Recreation Area. Continue on curving paved road 4.5 miles to campground.*

Closest Town: Las Cruces

Ownership: Bureau of Land Management (505) 525-4300

Wildlife watching along the east face of the Organ Mountains at Aguirre Spring is even better after sunset.
MARK NOHL/N M MAGAZINE

REGION 7: SOUTHERN MOUNTAINS

This region is a high, relatively cool "island" of mountain peaks surrounded by a sea of hot, dry plains. Sierra Blanca, a volcanic peak 11,977 feet above sea level, dominates the area, looming above the arid Tularosa Basin to the west. High forests of spruce, Douglas-fir, and pine gradually give way at lower elevations to pinon, alligator juniper, and Gambel oak. Wildlife of the region includes such species as the mountain lion, wild turkey, various hummingbirds, and shorebirds.

Photo, opposite page: Sierra Blanca. DON L. MacCARTER

Wildlife Viewing Sites

56. Valley of Fires
57. The Road to Sierra Blanca
58. Karr Canyon
59. Bluff Springs
60. Oliver Lee Memorial State Park
61. Holloman Lakes, White Sands
    National Monument

56 VALLEY OF FIRES

Description: Lava flowed in the Valley of Fires only yesterday in geologic time — about 1,500 years ago — making it one of the younger lava flows in the continental United States.

Viewing Information: Overlook at the Valley of Fires Recreation Area and a self-guiding, 0.5-mile nature trail. Gray-footed chipmunk, rock squirrel, brown towhee, and rock wren are common along the trail. Occasional viewing of desert mule deer, bobcat, coyote, kit fox, and ringtail. Exotic Barbary sheep inhabit the lava flow but are rarely seen. Watch for scaled quail, western kingbird, loggerhead shrike, black-throated sparrow, turkey vulture, and golden eagle. Watch for the melanistic wildlife of the area, whose dark-colored skin and fur variations let them blend in with the dark lava rock.

Directions: *From Carrizozo, travel west about 6 miles on U.S. Highway 380 to entrance on left.*

Closest Town: Carrizozo

Ownership: Bureau of Land Management (505) 648-2241

57 THE ROAD TO SIERRA BLANCA

Description: *AUTO TOUR.* A 9-mile drive through many life zones climbs to scenic 12,003-foot Sierra Blanca, a volcanic landmark visible for miles throughout southern New Mexico. Visibility at the Windy Point Vista Lookout stretches 100 miles or more on clear days. Round-trip drive to the lookout point and back is 18 miles.

Viewing Information: The Windy Point observation platform, with benches and barrier-free access, affords good year-round viewing of raptors, including turkey vulture, red-tailed hawk, and golden eagle, and bald eagle in winter. Wild turkey are often seen during spring courtship in the small roadside openings, generally along the upper half of the drive. Good viewing of elk spring through fall, with binoculars or a spotting scope, especially in early morning. Mountain lion are common in the area, though seldom seen.

Directions: *Just north of Ruidoso, start counting mileage at Alto where New Mexico Highway 532 heads up the mountain in a series of switchbacks. Watch for a broad, unmarked pullout on the left side of the road at 9.0 miles. This is the Windy Point Vista Overlook.*

Closest Town: Ruidoso

Ownership: USDA Forest Service (505) 257-4095

58 KARR CANYON

Description: At the edge of an area of farms, orchards, and country homes lies Karr Canyon, a small, ponderosa pine-studded valley bisected by an intermittent stream. A network of unmaintained trails crisscrosses this 100-acre site.

Viewing Information: Good birding area, especially in May for warblers; look for red-faced, Virginia's, Grace's and black-throated gray, as well as Cordilleran flycatcher, band-tailed pigeon, western bluebird, Steller's jay, and western tanager. Occasional sightings of blue grosbeak, lesser goldfinch, indigo bunting, long-tailed weasel, mule deer, raccoon, and elk, both at the site and en route through orchards and farms of the canyon. Best viewing times dawn/dusk, May through August.

Directions: *Travel 7 miles west of Cloudcroft on U.S. Highway 82 to the Karr Canyon Road sign, at milepost 9 near the village of High Rolls. Turn left and continue past brown sign for Karr Canyon Picnic Grounds. Paved road goes 4 miles— viewing area is located where road becomes gravel.*

Closest Town: High Rolls, Mountain Park

Ownership: USDA Forest Service (505) 682-2551

59 BLUFF SPRINGS

Description: Flowing over a cliff in a small, three-forked waterfall, the waters of Bluff Springs join the Rio Penasco at a particularly scenic spot. High-use area; visit mid-week for best viewing.

Viewing Information: Good dawn/dusk viewing of wild turkey in summer. Excellent viewing of broad-tailed and rufous hummingbird, especially in August when wildflowers are in full bloom. Good viewing of band-tailed pigeon, purple martin, green-tailed towhee, western tanager, mountain bluebird, ruby-crowned kinglet, numerous warbler species, red crossbill, and northern goshawk. Surrounding area is excellent Mexican spotted owl habitat.

Directions: *In Cloudcroft, turn south onto New Mexico Highway 130 and travel 1.7 miles. Turn right onto NM 6563 toward Sunspot. After 8.8 miles, turn left onto a paved road at the Bluff Springs sign. After 2 miles, the road becomes gravel and forks—take the left fork, which follows the Rio Penasco. Bluff Springs is on the right, 2 miles from end of pavement. A hiking trail leads off to left across the creek.*

Closest Town: Cloudcroft

Ownership: USDA Forest Service (505) 682-2551

60 OLIVER LEE MEMORIAL STATE PARK

Description: Surrounded by desert, this mico-habitat shelters a variety of wildlife. Along the west face of the Sacramento Mountains, the walls of Dog Canyon rise more than 2,000 vertical feet from the arid Tularosa Basin to the west. Freshwater springs, seeps in canyon walls, and a perennially-flowing stream and waterfall support a surprising amount of greenery.

Viewing Information: Watch for seasonal and resident birds, including canyon, Bewick's and cactus wren, great horned owl, mockingbird, broad-tailed and rufous hummingbird, ladder-backed woodpecker, curve-billed thrasher, Gambel's quail, greater roadrunner, mourning dove, northern oriole, and western tanager; best viewing between March 1 and July 31, in early morning. Look for mule deer, frequently seen in front of the visitor center, in early morning. Many other mammals are residents, though reclusive and hard to see. Best viewing times are early morning or late evening for coyote, kit fox, ringtail, and black-tailed jackrabbit. Occasional sightings of mountain lion. Viewing of gopher snake, black-tailed rattlesnake, wandering garter snake, and lizard species (Clark's spiny, tree, and side-blotched).

Directions: *From mid-town Alamogordo, continue on main thoroughfare (U.S. Highway 70) southwest for 1 mile. Turn left (south) onto U.S. 54. Continue 9 miles to park sign and turn left. Continue 4 miles to park entrance.*

Closest Town: Alamogordo

Ownership: New Mexico Park and Recreation Division (505) 437-8284

Although it doesn't nest at Oliver Lee State Park, the Rufous hummingbird is a frequent migratory visitor here. DON L. MacCARTER

Description: Holloman Lakes, which include a seasonally-dry playa and perennial Lake Holloman, is home to diverse migrating shorebirds and wintering waterfowl. Adjacent **White Sands National Monument** has nearly 300 square miles of shimmering white sand dunes.

Viewing Information: At Holloman Lakes, look along alkaline mudflats for nesting snowy plovers, black-necked stilts, and American avocets. Many sandpiper species, as well as long-billed dowitcher, greater and lesser yellowlegs, long-billed curlew, white-faced ibis, semipalmated plover, and Wilson's phalarope. Watch for Franklin's gull, also least and Forster's tern in April-May and August-September. Lakes contain treated wastewater unsuitable for human contact. Wildlife viewing **at White Sands** is generally subtle: look for tiny prints in the sand made by darkling beetles, snakes, lizards, and rodents. Keep a sharp eye out for the park's adapted "white" wildlife — good mid-morning viewing of bleached earless lizard; occasional sightings of kit fox, white pocket mice, and white insects, which tend to be nocturnal.

Directions: *From Alamogordo, go west on U.S. 70 for 7 miles to the western edge of Holloman Air Force Base; from here, it is 3 miles to the Lake Holloman Wildlife Habitat Area. Turn right at the sign and the Lake Stinky playa, following the gravel road 0.25 mile to Lake Holloman. Continue west 3 more miles on U.S. 70 to reach White Sands NM.*

Closest Town: Alamogordo

Ownership: *Holloman Lakes:* Lake Stinky managed by the Bureau of Land Management (505) 525-4300. Lake Holloman administered jointly by Holloman Air Force Base and BLM. Management coordinated with the Mesilla Valley Audubon Society. *White Sands National Monument:* National Park Service (505) 479-6124

*White Sands
National Monument is the
world's largest
gypsum
dune field.*
DON L. MacCARTER

REGION 8: STAKED PLAINS

The Llano Estacado (Staked Plains) extend westward from Texas into southeastern New Mexico. Some historians say early Spanish explorers drove stakes into the ground to find their way back across a trackless, flat plain. Others claim the soaptree yucca stalks looked like stakes. This region provides good habitat for waterfowl, as well as other species, such as the lesser prairie chicken, long-billed curlew, and the Mexican free-tailed bat.

Photo, opposite page: Staked Plains. **DON L. MacCARTER**

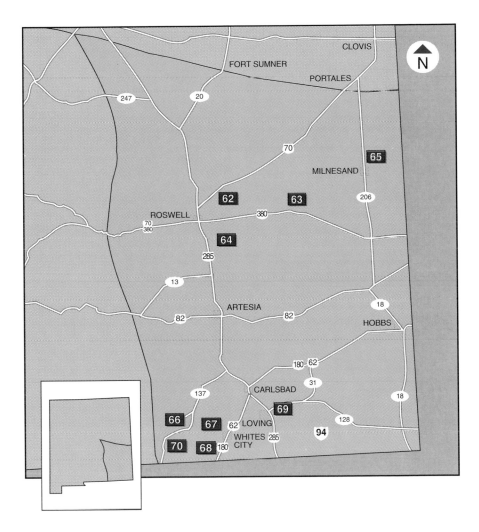

Wildlife Viewing Sites

62. Bitter Lake National Wildlife Refuge
63. Mescalero Sands
64. Bottomless Lakes State Park, Overflow Wetlands Wildlife Habitat Area
65. Black Hills and Milnesand Prairie Chicken Area

66. Sitting Bull Falls
67. Carlsbad Caverns National Park
68. Rattlesnake Springs
69. The Loving Heronries
70. Wilderness Ridge Drive

62 ◼ BITTER LAKE NATIONAL WILDLIFE REFUGE

Description: This viewing site is a winter home for migratory geese, ducks, lesser sandhill cranes, and other wildlife. The refuge contains 800-acre Bitter Lake, a natural playa, and 6 constructed lakes, as well as several marshes. Water levels fluctuate, but lakes are generally full by early winter. An 8.5-mile driving loop passes along lake and pond areas.

Viewing Information: November through mid-February, enjoy good viewing of 20,000-40,000 snow geese, along with several thousand Canada geese, puddle and diving ducks, and lesser sandhill cranes. Excellent fall viewing of migrating American white pelicans, with occasional sightings of ospreys. Various shore and wading birds may be seen year-round. A small colony of federally-listed endangered least terns nests here in summer. Watch for rattlesnakes during warmer months.

Directions: *Turn east onto New Mexico Highway 380 (Main Street) in Roswell. Drive 3 miles to the junction of NM 265. Turn north and continue 4 miles (Red Bridge Road). Turn right toward the Pecos River on East Pine Lodge Road for another 4 miles, following signs to refuge headquarters.*

Closest Town: Roswell

Ownership: U. S. Fish & Wildlife Service (505) 622-6755

63 ◼ MESCALERO SANDS

Description: This site offers viewing of a fascinating wildlife spectacle: the courtship ritual of the lesser prairie chicken. The male bird's extravagant display, designed to attract a mate, involves bowing, drumming its feet, spinning, and sparring with rival males. Dancing occurs from early March through mid-May, with peak activity in April, when hens arrive.

Viewing Information: Male birds begin their courtship about one half hour before sunrise. Plan on a two-hour observation span. Contact the BLM Roswell Resource Area office for best dates and areas to visit. Occasional viewing of pronghorn and mule deer, as well as ladder-backed woodpecker, loggerhead shrike, mourning dove, scaled quail, and Swainson's hawk. The massassagua rattlesnake is also common here.

Directions: *From downtown Roswell, take U.S. Highway 380 east for 46 miles to the Mescalero Sands Recreation Area on south side of highway, then proceed 2 miles east to the Walldrip Rest Area. Turn left (north) immediately across from the rest area to enter the Caprock Wildlife Habitat Area.*

Closest Town: Roswell

Ownership: Bureau of Land Management (505) 624-1790; New Mexico State Land Office (505) 827-5033

BOTTOMLESS LAKES STATE PARK, OVERFLOW WETLANDS WILDLIFE HABITAT AREA

Description: These 7 sinkhole lakes, each filled with crystalline, blue-green water, were formed when groundwater dissolved salt and gypsum to form subterranean caverns. When the roofs of the caverns collapsed, sinkholes were formed. Overflow Wetlands, located south of and adjacent to the park, is an important riparian-wetland area of the Pecos River for migratory waterfowl.

Viewing Information: Very good shorebird and general birding area. Excellent viewing of migrating snow geese, northern pintail, American wigeon, gadwall, mallard, teal species, canvasback, and northern shoveler, as well as sandhill cranes and Canada geese at the Overflow Wetlands and on Lazy Lagoon in the park. Best viewing at the Overflow Wetlands is just after sunrise, September through February. Occasional year-round viewing of greater roadrunner, jackrabbit, mule deer, and raccoon. The barking frog can be heard (but rarely seen) during thunderstorms May through August; also resident here are the yellow mud turtle and Couch's spadefoot toad. Avoid weekend, holiday, summer and afternoon visits; at these times, visit nearby Bitter Lake NWR.

Directions: *Travel 12 miles east of Roswell on U.S. Highway 380 to top of bluff, then turn south onto New Mexico Highway 409 and travel about 3 miles to state park entrance. To reach Overflow Wetlands, go to Lea Lake area of the park and continue south for 3.5 miles. Turn right onto a dirt road for 1.75 miles and park. From this site, a crane roost can be observed to the west. Visitors may hike up the road to the central ponds to view waterfowl from hilltop.*

Closest Town: Roswell

Ownership: New Mexico Park & Recreation Division (505) 624-6058; Bureau of Land Management (505) 624-1790; New Mexico State Land Office (505) 827-5033

Snow geese occur in two color phases in New Mexico, white and "blue." The Ross' goose, a separate, smaller species, flocks together with snow geese at this and other sites.
JIM CLARK

65 BLACK HILLS AND MILNESAND PRAIRIE CHICKEN AREA

Description: These sites, located in the midst of dry-land agriculture country, still support active courting grounds, or *leks*, of the lesser prairie chicken. Reddish sand hills, studded with bunchgrass, shinnery oak, and oil rigs, roll on to the eastern horizon. Caliche gravel roads wind through the property. No facilities at this site; bring water.

Viewing Information: Excellent viewing of the courtship of the lesser prairie chicken from about March 15 through April 20. Listen for the "booming" sounds created by male birds as they expel air from the brightly-colored sacs on their throats, and drum the ground with their feet. A good way to locate active leks is to arrive in the pre-dawn darkness. Remain in vehicle; open windows and listen for the booming or drumming sounds of male birds. Drive slowly until locating their calls. Stay in vehicle or use a blind—the birds will completely ignore visitors. Best viewing times are just before sunrise to about 7 a.m., although times can vary. Recreational visitors at lands administered by New Mexico State Land Office are not allowed within 500 feet of oil and gas drilling rigs and other equipment.

Directions: *Travel south of Portales about 32 miles on New Mexico Highway 206. Watch for small signs on both sides of the highway, saying "Black Hills Prairie Chicken Area." The road to the left (east) leads into the dunes area. Access to the Milnesand site is available 3.5 miles due east of Milnesand, where a dirt road turns south for 2 miles, jogs east 0.5 mile, then turns south again to the site. Another access is 5 miles south of Milnesand at the Roosevelt County line where a gated (but unlocked) road heads east 3.5 miles to the site. The many dirt roads on site are unmarked and constantly subject to alteration by oil companies.*

Closest Town: Portales

Ownership: New Mexico State Land Office (505) 827-5033; some portions managed in cooperation with New Mexico Dept. of Game & Fish (505) 624-6135

In spring, lesser prairie chickens display a colorful courtship ritual. Males puff out air sacs on their throats and spread their wings as they strut.
LARRY BROCK

Description: This scenic oasis in the Chihuahuan Desert lies in the midst of canyon country where mesquite and yucca grow. Within a steep-walled, semi-circular basin, water creates a micro-habitat of lush vegetation in which madrone, willow, bigtooth maple, and oak thrive. An upper and lower falls bring water into clear, green rock pools below. Rimmed with willows, rushes and reeds, these pools provide habitat for a variety of wildlife. Last Chance Canyon hiking trail begins 1 mile before the entrance to Sitting Bull Falls at Forest Road 276B; park at trailhead 0.25 mile west of blacktop. This 4-mile trail leads to large, ever-flowing Last Chance Spring.

Viewing Information: Very good viewing of canyon wren, western and hepatic tanager, Cassin's kingbird, white-throated swift, black-headed and blue grosbeak, black phoebe, and other songbirds mid-April through October. Good year-round viewing of rock squirrel, black-tailed jackrabbit, ringtail, and mule deer. Mountain lion sign is abundant at Last Chance Spring. Best viewing at Sitting Bull Falls mid-week only, early morning and late evening—site becomes crowded weekends and holidays. Visit spring and fall for most comfortable viewing. Summer temperatures regularly exceed 100 degrees.

Directions: From Carlsbad, take U.S. Highway 285 north 12 miles to New Mexico Highway 137. Drive 31 miles to junction with County Road 409. Take right fork, and follow signs 8 miles to Sitting Bull Falls. Turnoff to Last Chance Canyon occurs at dirt road on right, at the 7-mile mark.

Closest Town: Carlsbad

Ownership: USDA Forest Service 885-4181

Sitting Bull Falls is a micro-habitat of lush vegetation and clear, green water in the Chihuahuan Desert. DON L. MacCARTER

67 CARLSBAD CAVERNS NATIONAL PARK

Description: Beneath the Chihuahuan Desert's rugged mountains and broad plains lies the subterranean world of Carlsbad Caverns. The vast chambers and unique mineral formations here remain at a constant temperature of 56 degrees. Several forms of wildlife live in or at the mouth of the caverns, while other species frequent the above-ground terrain.

Viewing Information: On the road to the caverns, enjoy good viewing of desert mule deer year-round. Also watch for the nocturnal ringtail and hognose skunk between 9 p.m. and 11 p.m. on summer evenings, and raccoons near the amphitheater area. Excellent viewing of two species at the mouth of the caverns: by day, see the largest nesting colony of cave swallows in the United States from March 1 through October 15; at dusk, watch the exit flight of nearly 1 million Mexican free-tailed bats as they leave for a night of feasting on insects. Bats are best seen May through October. The bat flight spectacle can be viewed from the outdoor amphitheater at the cave's natural entrance. Ranger-led talks on the bats usually start about 7 p.m; inquire at the information desk for exact times.

Directions: *From Carlsbad, take U.S. Highway 62/180 south of Carlsbad about 20 miles to Whites City. Turn right at the sign to the park at CR 7 and climb about 7 miles to park headquarters.*

Closest Town: Whites City

Ownership: National Park Service (505) 785-2232

Nearly one million Mexican free-tailed bats leave the natural entrance of Carlsbad Caverns at twilight to feast on insects above the adjacent plains.
CARLSBAD CAVERNS

Description: The fenced, riparian portion of this site is home to many birds; a footpath has been worn beside the water. Rattlesnake Springs is managed by The Nature Conservancy; a National Park Service picnic area adjoins the site.

Viewing Information: Very good seasonal viewing of yellow-billed cuckoo, vermillion flycatcher, Chihuahuan raven, eastern bluebird, Bell's vireo, summer tanager, bunting species—painted, indigo, and varied—also green-backed heron, orchard oriole, northern cardinal, and many other species. Up to 200 turkey vultures have been known to roost here; best viewing times and numbers occur mid-August to mid-September. Spring and fall afford comfortable temperatures for viewing; summer temperatures regularly exceed 100 degrees.

Directions: *From Carlsbad, take U.S. Highway 62/180 south about 26 miles. Turn right onto County Road 418 and follow signs 3 miles to picnic area.*

Closest Town: Carlsbad

Ownership: The Nature Conservancy (505) 988-3867; National Park Service (505) 785-2232

Turkey vultures are colloquially called "buzzards." These carrion feeders are recognized in flight by the shallow V-formation of their wings.
LARRY BROCK

69 THE LOVING HERONRIES

Description: A series of salt lakes on sagebrush flats east of Loving is the site of several active nesting colonies for herons and egrets. No facilities.

Viewing Information: Mid-May to mid-June, watch for black-crowned night herons, snowy egrets, cattle egrets, one or two pairs of little blue herons, and rare sightings of the tricolored heron. These birds may be seen roosting and nesting in dead salt cedars near the lakes. Best viewing from 5 p.m. to dusk, when birds fly to and from the nearby Pecos River to the west. Dunlins are present in April, snowy plovers late March through September; occasional black-necked stilts April through August, with best viewing in June.

Directions: *From the "Y" intersection of U.S. Highway 285 and U.S. 62/180 in Carlsbad, drive south on U.S. 285 about 9 miles. Turn left (east) onto New Mexico Highway 31. Continue about 7.5 miles and turn right on NM 128. Travel 0.6 mile past mile marker 1, and turn left through a gate. Continue on dirt road a short distance and turn onto a faint dirt track to the right. Track leads to an abandoned oil pad. From here, look to the east for the closest heronry.*

Closest Town: Loving

Ownership: Bureau of Land Management (505) 887-6544

With its black bill and yellow feet, the snowy egret stirs up mud to flush its prey.
JOHN AND KAREN
HOLLINGSWORTH

Description: *AUTO TOUR.* A gravel road follows a steep, forested ridge in the Guadalupe Mountains near the Texas state line. Devil's Den hiking trail, a rough, 5-mile trek, can be accessed about 2 miles before the end of the road; the trail leads to a rock spring under maple, oak, and pine trees. At the end of the road is dramatic McKittrick Canyon Overlook. Late October to mid-November brings a blaze of autumn color to the canyon, with its high, sheer walls, diversity of trees, and spring-fed stream. Plan on a half-day to complete this drive.

Viewing Information: Occasional summer viewing of golden eagle, owl species, turkey vulture, band-tailed pigeon, white-throated swift, gray flycatcher, western bluebird, hepatic tanager, and rufous-sided towhee. Mexican spotted owl and whip-poor-will occasionally heard. View rattlesnakes spring through fall; gray fox, porcupine, ringtail, gray-footed chipmunk, rock squirrel, mule deer, and occasional wild turkey year-round. Sightings of elk and black bear. Look for mountain lion sign; this area supports a large population.

Directions: *From Carlsbad, take U.S. Highway 285 north 12 miles to New Mexico Highway 137. Turn left onto NM 137 for about 44 miles to the settlement of Queen. After passing the Queen Store on right, continue 4 miles to FR 540, marked "Overlook," and follow road south; continue 11.5 miles to FR201. FOUR-WHEEL-DRIVE VEHICLES ONLY FROM FR201. Continue 1.5 miles to overlook; although road continues, stop here.*

Closest Town: Queen

Ownership: USDA Forest Service (505) 885-4181

A bobcat generally leads a solitary life, except when it's a kitten, cared for by its mother, and again as an adult during breeding. DON L. MacCARTER

REGION 9: GREATER BOOTHEEL

The southwestern corner of New Mexico is known as The Bootheel, because the state boundary looks like the heel of a cowboy boot. Although this region appears (and can be) harsh and forbidding, it offers pockets of surprising beauty, some of which are open to the public, and others which remain private, including the famous Gray Ranch. This region is excellent habitat for a variety of reptile species, including the Gila monster and checkered whiptail lizard. Uncommon birds, such as the zone-tailed hawk and elegant trogon, may also be found here. Many mammal species, such as the desert bighorn sheep, thrive in this harsh environment.

Photo, opposite page: Animas Mountains. **GARY RASMUSSEN**

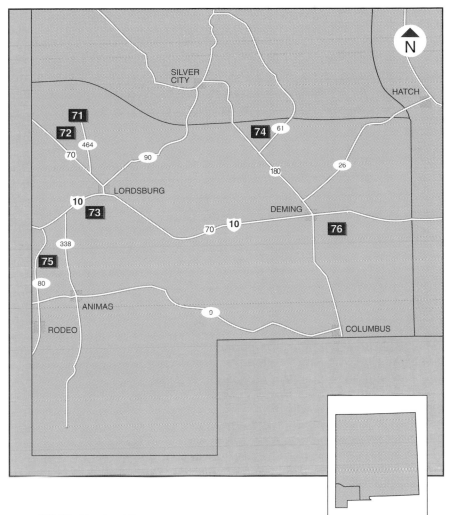

Wildlife Viewing Sites

71. Rock Rock Wildlife Area
72. Lower Gila Box
73. Lordsburg Playas
74. City of Rocks State Park
75. Granite Gap
76. Spring Canyon (Rock Hound State Park)

71 RED ROCK WILDLIFE AREA

Description: With its rocky hills, nearby mountains, and the Gila River, this remote site is prime habitat for desert bighorn sheep, a diversity of birds, and other wildlife. A 1,250-acre enclosure maintained by the New Mexico Department of Game and Fish serves as a propagation and research facility for desert bighorn sheep. No facilities at this site.

Viewing Information: Excellent year-round viewing of desert bighorn sheep on cliffs when they are near the roadside portion of the enclosure. Occasional viewing of mule deer, javelina, and coyote. Arrangements can be made to visit an adjacent wetland site with excellent birding on Game Dept. property—call (505) 542-9760 at least 3 days in advance of visit. *VIEW SHEEP FROM ROADSIDES ONLY. DO NOT ENTER ENCLOSURE; VIOLATORS ARE PROSECUTED.*

Directions: *From Lordsburg, travel north on U.S. Highway 70 for 2 miles. Turn right onto New Mexico Highway 464 and continue 23 miles to the Gila River. Take first right after crossing river onto Game Department Road. Continue 2.6 miles to sign on right for New Mexico Department of Game and Fish. This is a private residence and, the entrance to wetland area—do not turn in here unless arrangements have been made (see above section). Continue 2 miles along Game Department Road to southern boundary of sheep enclosure. ROAD IMPASSABLE IN WET WEATHER.*

Closest Town: Lordsburg

Ownership: New Mexico Dept. of Game and Fish (505) 827-9904 or 542-9760

New Mexico's desert bighorn population numbers about 300, with 80 at the Red Rock Wildlife Area and 220 inhabiting other southwestern mountain ranges.
DON L. MacCARTER

Description: This quiet stretch of the Gila River has a broad, sandy beach, and shady groves of cottonwood, Arizona sycamore, and hackberry beneath the rocky cliffs that form the Lower Box. A good site for viewing nesting raptors. *FUEL UP, BRING WATER AND PROVISIONS—NO SERVICES BEYOND LORDSBURG.*

Viewing Information: Excellent viewing of wildlife tracks in the sand — from insects to reptiles, birds to mammals. Excellent viewing of Gambel's and scaled quail on the road to the site. Other birds here include the vermillion flycatcher, common black hawk, green-backed heron, gray and Bell's vireo, painted red-start, northern cardinal, cliff swallow, canyon wren, black-throated sparrow, and white-winged dove; best viewing spring through fall. Occasional year-round viewing of mule deer and coyote. Rare sightings of bobcat, black bear, and mountain lion. Excellent viewing of reptiles, including spiny softshell turtle, and greater earless and Clark's spiny lizard. May through October, look for western diamondback and black-tailed rattlesnake. This is a wilderness study area. Stay on existing trails; no cross-country motorized travel allowed.

Directions: *Travel north of Lordsburg U.S. Highway 70 for 2 miles, and turn right on New Mexico Highway 464. Travel 14.1 miles to a point 50 feet south of the Grant County/Hidalgo County boundary sign. Turn left (west) on the only dirt road in the vicinity. Drive 3.6 miles and turn right (north) at the first gravel cross-road. Continue another 4.9 miles to the sign for site; continue 0.8 mile to river.*

Closest Town: Lordsburg

Ownership: Bureau of Land Management (505) 525-4300

The common black hawk's name is very misleading. This seldom-seen bird, which is often mistaken for a vulture, is quite rare in New Mexico.
HELEN AND NOEL SNYDER

73 LORDSBURG PLAYAS

Description: Once part of ancient Pleistocene waters, these broad, shallow lakes occur seasonally over an alkali pan. Alkali sacaton grass grows around the perimeter of the brackish playa waters. No facilities at this site.

Viewing Information: An occasional stopping place for migratory waterfowl, especially in September. Look for sporadic numbers of mallard, northern pintail, northern shoveler, numerous sandpipers, dowitcher, yellowlegs, American avocet, and rare sightings of long-billed curlew. Viewing of western gull species. Look for the plains spadefoot toad and yellow mud turtle. During spring and fall migration, birds feed here on fairy and tadpole shrimp.

Directions: *From Lordsburg, go west on I-10 for about five miles to the Gary Exit. Turn right (north) and follow the railroad tracks left (west) until you can cross over. Continue west until you can see the water. Do not drive too close, since the clay mud can be extremely sticky. Note: The pond at the No. 11 Animas freeway exit (NM 338) has water all year; however, it is privately owned and viewing is from the highway shoulder only.*

Closest Town: Lordsburg

Ownership: Bureau of Land Management, (505) 525-4300; New Mexico State Land Office, (505) 827-5033; Some private lands

74 CITY OF ROCKS STATE PARK

Description: This remote state park is a natural "Stonehenge" of unusual volcanic rock formations more than 30 million years old. Be sure to take the 0.25-mile Observation Point Road at the park for a good view of the area.

Viewing Information: Spring and fall dawn/dusk viewing is best here; summer temperatures routinely exceed 100 degrees. Occasional year-round viewing of scaled and Gambel's quail, greater roadrunner, rock squirrel, black-tailed jackrabbit, porcupine, coyote, kangaroo rat, and snakes. Great horned owls have nested in rock crevices here. April through November, look for western diamondback and prairie rattlesnakes.

Directions: *From Silver City, take U.S. Highway 180 southeast about 23 miles to the junction with New Mexico Highway 61. Turn left (northeast) onto NM 61 and continue 3 miles to City of Rocks Road and park entrance.*

Closest Town: Hurley

Ownership: New Mexico Park and Recreation Department (505) 536-2800; New Mexico State Land Office (505) 827-5033

Description: From surrounding flat country, spectacular granite and lime-stone ridges and rock formations rise up to encircle a secluded bowl of land near the Arizona border. This is an excellent example of Chihuahuan Desert vegetation. Look for flowering ocotillo, cactus, agave, and wildflowers in season. *FUEL UP, BRING PROVISIONS AND WATER BEFORE VISITING—NO SERVICES AVAILABLE.*

Viewing Information: Excellent viewing of a variety of lizards and other reptiles, including rattlesnakes. Occasional viewing of the rare Gila monster. Very good viewing of curve-billed and Bendire's thrasher, black-throated sparrow, cactus and rock wren, northern mockingbird, verdin, greater roadrunner, hummingbird species, Gambel's quail, and northern harrier spring through fall. Occasional year-round sightings of nocturnal ringtail, desert bighorn sheep, javelina, mule deer, and coyote.

Directions: *Travel 15 miles west of Lordsburg on Interstate 10 and take exit 5 (Road Forks). Drive south on New Mexico Highway 80 and turn right after 11 miles onto an unmarked dirt track. At the entrance, there will be a wire gate between two wooden posts—BE SURE TO CLOSE GATE AFTER ENTERING PROPERTY. Take left fork and park near the first large rock cluster. Do not drive past the cut in the rocks. Sandy road stretch is about 0.5 mile. ROAD IMPASSABLE IN WET WEATHER.*

Closest Town: Road Forks

Ownership: Bureau of Land Management (505) 525-4300

Researchers have implanted minature radio transmitters in the abdomens of some Gila monsters, in order to locate their shelters, monitor movement, and discover other biological data. DON L. MacCARTER

76 SPRING CANYON (ROCK HOUND STATE PARK)

Description: This park, a developed day-use site with amenities, provides access to the rugged terrain of the Florida Mountains. A mountain hiking trail begins at the picnic area. The park is open 8 a.m. to 7 p.m., closed Mondays and Tuesdays, and in winter. Best visiting times are spring and fall, since summer temperatures often climb above 100 degrees.

Viewing Information: Look for exotic Persian ibex, wild goats introduced to this area during the 1970s. Ibex are commonly seen year-round in the surrounding hills and cliffs. Also watch for mule deer, ringtail, gray fox, rock squirrel, and bats. Mountain lions are numerous, though elusive and rarely seen. Good birding for raptors, quail, dove, hummingbirds, and songbirds. The park abounds with reptiles, including four species of rattlesnake, various other snakes, horned and other toad species, and numerous lizards. Beautiful spring wildflower displays in the foothills.

Directions: *From Deming, travel 4 miles south on New Mexico Highway 11 to the junction of NM141. Turn left (east) and continue 8 miles to the junction of NM143. Turn right, following NM143 to the junction with NM198. Turn right, following pavement to park entrance.*

Closest Town: Deming

Ownership: New Mexico Park and Recreation Division (505) 546-6182

New Mexico's state bird is the greater roadrunner, an omnivore which feeds on lizards, insects, and small birds and mammals. JOHN AND KAREN HOLLINGSWORTH

WILDLIFE INDEX

The following index identifies wildlife species noted in this guide, followed by the site numbers where they may be viewed.